Parish Planning
A Practical Guide to
Shared Responsibility

Robert G. Howes

A Liturgical Press Book

THE LITURGICAL PRESS
Collegeville, Minnesota

Cover design by David Manahan, O.S.B.

1	2	3	4	5	6	7	8

Library of Congress Cataloging-in-Publication Data

Howes, Robert G. (Robert Gerard), 1919–
    Parish planning : a practical guide to shared responsibility / Robert G. Howes.
        p.   cm.
    "A Liturgical Press book."
    ISBN 0-8146-2165-1
    1. Parish councils.   2. Catholic Church—Government.   3. Clergy.
  4. Lay ministry.   I. Title.
    BX1920.H69   1994
    254'.0273—dc20   94-7251
                                                 CIP

CONTENTS

FOREWORD

From its very beginning, the Church has been revealed to be a community of people formed by the Word of God, animated by the creative power of the Holy Spirit, and sustained by the worship and service of its members. Its mission is both to proclaim the message of Christ for the enlightenment of the hearts and minds of people and to provide a place where his healing presence can be experienced. As such, the Church must always understand itself as existing not for itself but for the world. The Church, therefore, is called to be a community of ministers charged with the task of bringing the healing presence of Christ to a wounded humanity.

This responsibility of being about the work of Christ's Church is ours, regardless of our state in life or the differing roles we may exercise. We are called to be co-creators with God, advancing the Kingdom in our day. Every person's contribution is vitally needed so that together in a rich diversity we can build up the Christian community by enhancing the sacredness and growth of others. Responsibility for the mission of the Church is collaborative and is shared by all the baptized, all bound together by a variety of gifts and ministries, and all serving the one priestly mission of our Lord Jesus Christ.

The parish is the center of the Church's life, the place where Christians gather to hear the Word, to celebrate the

Eucharist and other sacramental rites of the Church, to support one another in faith and in the face of personal and social challenges, and to become energized for mission both to the Church community and to the wider society and world. Today our parishes are faced with many challenges: the dramatic reduction of priest and religious personnel; the increasing secularism in our society; shifting populations from our cities to our suburbs; immigration of Hispanics and Asians, to cite just a few.

There are certain times in the life of the world and the Church when the Holy Spirit has been poured forth abundantly, creating a new vision and a new horizon which gives shape and direction to humankind and civilization for generations to come. We, I believe, are living in precisely such an age, in a new Pentecost; and, as a priestly people, we have a golden opportunity to become involved at the heart of this reawakening, of being forerunners of the Church of tomorrow.

Good pastoral planning enables us to read and interpret the signs of our times and is essential if we are to insure the best utilization of our human, physical, and fiscal resources as today we lay the foundations for the parishes of tomorrow. Fr. Robert Howes' timely book outlines practical and tested ways for parishes to conduct effective pastoral planning which will produce lasting results. The ideas developed in this book evolve from Father Howes' many years of pioneering and invaluable experience working in a variety of dioceses and parishes throughout the United States and Canada. Father Howes aptly stresses that effective planning occurs when it is done *with the people* rather than only *for them.* In his chapter entitled *The Quantity Imperative,* he describes ways to make this happen.

Father Howes addresses the key elements contained in sound pastoral planning: data gathering with both the objective facts and subjective feelings, ownership, accountability, evaluation, setting priorities, and the role of the pastor and parish leaders. This book will be a real treasure for those in parish leadership as it provides a structure through which parish leaders can channel their own insights, experience, and creativity as they set directions today for the parish and Church of tomorrow.

✝ Howard J. Hubbard
Bishop of Albany
March 8, 1993

(Bishop Hubbard is the episcopal liaison person between the National Conference of Catholic Bishops and the Conference for Pastoral Planning and Council Development.)

ACKNOWLEDGMENTS

While I am, of course, totally accountable for the ideas in this text, I am most grateful to those who have helped or simply been patient en route. I thank my colleagues in the National Pastoral Planning Conference and in the Conference for Pastoral Planning and Council Development, Bishop Hubbard for his perceptive introduction and friendship, Archbishop Levada and Bishop Imesch for their wisdoms as I consulted with them, and indeed all the bishops and archbishops with whom I have been privileged to minister in the past quarter century. A special note of appreciation is offered to Fathers Whit Evans in Duluth and Scotty MacDonald in Manchester for their suggestions. Finally, I thank my secretary with whose assistance the text marched to finality—Ms. Cathleen Corbett of Portland. At base, though, my gratitude goes to my good parents, to the Sulpicians and Jesuits who taught me, to the city and regional planning faculty at the Massachusetts Institute of Technology, and with much enthusiasm to the then Bishop John Wright of Worcester who first encouraged me to develop my interest in community relations to the point where, ultimately, this book became possible. Thanks to all of these and to those many others I met along the way as I vikinged across North America. SKOAL!

OVERVIEW

This book begins with a statement of how and why this author proposes to write yet another book on the contemporary North American parish.

It continues with a thorough inquiry into the Quantity Imperative, in two dimensions, as an essential ingredient in effective planning.

Next it moves into the RECKON ROAD. This acronym describes the author's updated and expanded parish planning methodology. Each step along the road is specified and exemplified.

Then a description is given for how a parish without a plan can take charge of its challenges.

Finally, specific foci shift to the two principal actors in the parish planning drama—its pastor and its council.

CHAPTER ONE

THE WHYS and the WHEREFORES

ANOTHER BOOK?

Views on and tentatives in the contemporary North American parish are already multitudinous. Views on and practices of *planagement** are, if anything, even more multitudinous. On the shelves in one bookstore in Portland recently I counted more than one hundred books, audio and visual cassettes in the subject area! They ranged all the way from "The Leadership Secrets of Attila the Hun" through Drucker and "Excellence" to Deming and Japan. Why, then, another book? There are several whys:

1. There is so much and such diverse material. This book analyzes and coheres a lot of it. This book begins at least to demonstrate and annotate the amplitude of these resources and the benefits which can accrue to an alert parish from a judicious use of them.

Planagement is the title of a book published by the American Management Association and written by Robert M. Randolph, director of the Professional Management Institute in Tulsa, Oklahoma in 1975. It proposes that planning and management are so interconnected that one word best describes them. Pastoral planning is similarly an umbrella term. It encompasses, as does *planagement*, not only planning and management strictly so called but also cybernetics, systems, organizational development etc. Thus throughout this text when I use the word *planagement* or the term pastoral planning I intend always this kind of comprehensive spread.

2. To establish a good relationship between ideas and practices in secular *planagement* and the Church in its parishes requires close familiarity with these ideas and practices. Simply to skim through a few texts and study a few methodologies cannot suffice. I hold a graduate degree in City and Regional Planning from the Massachusetts Institute of Technology. I have been a charter member of the American Institute of Certified Planners. For seven years I organized and directed the accredited graduate degree program in Planning at the Catholic University of America. For three years I coordinated the Department for Church Management and Organization at the Center for Applied Research in the Apostolate (CARA). I was vice president in the human resources consulting firm of Dr. Felix M. Lopez. I was a senior associate of Mr. Randolph. I have thus kept continuously close to the literature and developments in *planagement*. I claim no final or total wisdom. I launch these pages from a somewhat unique understanding of the secular disciplines to which I here relate the parochial Church. Indeed, I see myself as a trained secular and religious professional in many ways summoned to the kind of broad accountability identified ten years ago by a new university chancellor

> (I have) a fundamental responsibility to understand change, to look for trades, to question assumptions, to dream better ways, to talk, to listen, to connect our philosophical, ethical and cultural heritage with the science and technology that is pushing us forward . . . into the 21st century. The challenge of liberal education in the future is to connect the humanities with the sciences and technology that are transforming our modern world.[1]

3. To establish a good relationship between the Church as parish and secular *planagement* requires close familiarity with that Church. As a professional and peripatetic pastoral planner, I have in the past quarter century con-

sulted with more than thirty American and Canadian (arch)dioceses. I am a diocesan priest. In 1966 and 1967 I directed the Baltimore Urban Parish Study from which emerged one of the first two planning offices in an American chancery. I was, in 1972, a founder of the National (Catholic) Pastoral Planning Conference. I have published and conducted workshops widely in the Church. Again I claim neither final nor total wisdom. I launch these pages with a somewhat unique and hands-on experience of the North American Church.

It may be argued, however, that there is little theology in these pages. The point is valid but the likely conclusion from it is invalid. What I propose to do here is not canon law. It is not theology, unless, perhaps, theology with hands and feet. But I in no way denigrate or underestimate the respective roles of canon law and theology in the life of a parish. I simply recommend in professional detail ideas and practices which can more effectively enlarge from and activate them in the contemporary parochial circumstance—in the manner of flesh complementing spirit! Back in 1970–71, a canonist Father Bill Bassett, and I published companion articles on area vicariates in *The Jurist*. The articles complemented each other. His was entirely canonical and thus, I suppose, theological; mine was entirely secular and existential. I reflected on all the personal and corporate dimensions and quandaries surrounding middle management at the regional level. This, I suggest, made much sense. Indeed, the Church today would do well to emulate what we did. There are many situations in our policies and polities which are not subject, on the one hand, only to canon law and theology or, on the other hand, only to appropriate secular sciences. For us, as for business and civics, what is most urgent with increasing frequency is an interdisciplinary perspective rather than a narrow disciplinary bias. In any case, if this text is neither canonical nor theological (in the traditional sense of that term), it is deliberately calculated to undergird those judgments which an alert contemporary parish makes in these areas as it grows in grace and wisdom.

4. Like everything and everyone else, *planagement* is not static. Simply to skim through a few texts in a fixed timeframe cannot suffice. To develop an effective interface between parochial ecclesiology and these secular disciplines requires a close awareness of growth and change at both poles. True, there are still giants in *planagement* who stand greatly relevant—like Frederick Taylor, Rensis Likert, Peter Drucker, Douglas MacGregor, etc.! But there are all sorts of new and developing insights and the end is not in sight. A few examples: Where before we *planagers* often saw ourselves as philosopher kings (and queens) and were therefore supremely self-confident, now the situation is much more complex and we "plan *with* people" not just *for* them. Whereas before we too basked in "prosperity" and assured "progress," now we confront "austerity" and much "cynicism." We don't write "master plans" anymore. We too nibble at tomorrow! We too, as the fog level rises around us, drive more slowly and our horizons shorten. In the Church also there is flux. The initial euphorias of Vatican II have dimmed considerably. We have found, often painfully, that merely to decree *aggiornamento* (update) does not make it happen. In short, these pages explicitly acknowledge and reckon with much fluidity. Parishes, when they propose to profit from *planagement*, need to be *au courant* at both poles. I claim neither total nor final wisdom. I do bring to this text a somewhat unique understanding of such fluidity.

5. Under our steeples as elsewhere, there is too often a tendency to equate PAPERS and PROCESS with *planagement* success. Indeed, this tendency afflicts churches and other nonprofits even more than it does business and

civics. We neglect the *transfer factor,* i.e., how to get what has been planned done with these people here, now, and the day after tomorrow. I am a design planner. We design planners focus from the outset precisely on this transfer factor. My own logo FROM INSIGHT TO IMPACT evidences this. We do need prayer. We do need "research." But we need also to advance from our pious PAPERS and PROCESS into consequence, into outcomes. I have found, however, that far too many church leaders content themselves with elaborate insights. In the thrill of nice meetings and noble documents, they fail to wheel into place structures and tactics which alone enable these good intentions to become reality. A major purpose of this text is thus to indicate ways in which we can more effectively accommodate the transfer factor.

ORGANIZATIONAL ILLITERATES?

There is another rationale behind these pages. Nearly a quarter century ago, a prominent Catholic sociologist said that "most churchmen, the decision makers, are sociologically illiterate."[2] A few years later, I wrote:

> We have too often been theoretical, tall-in-our-dream-tower Christians. . . . (We have been fearful lest) by better tooling up our structures and informing our leaders in secular wisdoms, we destroy their inspiration and impede their graces.[3]

Hyperbole? Perhaps. But we did seem to canonize an adage which read: "sloppiness is next to godliness." So long as we prayed and were generically good, to be managerially wise was a kind of aberration:

> 20 years ago "management" was a bad word in non-profit institutions. It meant "big business." Far too many of these institutions believed that good intentions and a noble cause are all that is needed to produce good results. . . . (Non-profits) thought there was no need to "manage" because

(they had) no "bottom line." More and more of them have
since learned that they have to manage especially well precisely because they lack the discipline of a bottom line.[4]

To the extent that such organizational illiteracy existed before Vatican II it made little matter. We thrived. Pews and
seminaries were full. There was no talk of austerity in lean
chanceries. Much was, however, accomplished. Indeed, I
stand in constant awe and gratitude when I reflect on how
much was done in our dioceses and parishes by pious but
largely untrained amateurs! But then things changed. We
were immersed, as was the nation, in a revolution of instant expectations. We moved into a "People of God" polity. We became circles not pyramids. We confronted drastic
clergy shortages. We wrestled with massive diversities both
in our rectories and in our pews. We have at least somewhat adjusted to all of this. But still if we are no longer "illiterate" we remain far short of the professional excellence
which our contemporary situation requires. This book is
intended to help us as we mature.

PERSPECTIVE: THE WHEREFORES

> We are in a position to reflect on our experience. . . Now
> we can know. . . . Now we can debate, not in a theoreti-
> cal vacuum but on the basis of . . . experience.[5]

My perspective as I ponder this experience invokes three
cardinal principles:

a. *No parish is an organization, but every parish has an
   organization.* Parishes and everyone/everything in them
   are subject to "the human condition":

> Although the church has a divine commission it is a very
> human organization. This means that it is encumbered with
> all the weaknesses and frailties that accompany every other
> human organization. . . . The local church is a highly com-
> plex institution.[6]

If this has always been so, it is increasingly so today. We pluralize in a bewildered and bewildering world. We must "get organized for . . . ministry and mission in a new and uncertain environment."[7] We must manage our deliberately participative missions through fallible and finite persons, budgets, committees, clocks, and buildings. In short:

> The Church cannot operate without organization or structure. Even the Apostles assigned leadership, delegated work, shared responsibility and organized efforts for the good of the growing Christian community.[8]

As the number of active clergy ages and declines and as lay ministries multiply and the expectations of our parishioners increase, this urgency for good *planagement* in every one of our parishes likewise grows.

b. *Participation and planning are two sides of the same pastoral coin.* Put otherwise, when one is crippled, the other limps. In these pages, I swing back and forth between these two necessarily linked concerns.

c. *Effectiveness = performance + satisfaction.* The ultimate aim of all *planagement* is to increase effectiveness. A parish is effective only when it does more and more good things better and when more and more of its people feel involved and fulfilled in the process. Thus, both in the way it shares and in the way it plans, it must at once perform and satisfy.

Each of these principles must work through a complex reality. There will be a good deal of euphoria as the effort begins. Once a parish is resolved, it may seem just a matter of collectively walking its talk. But pious intentions cannot suffice. Much patience, courage, and perseverance will be required. When organizations start to "plan with people," often they find themselves in an affective dualism. There may well be (at) the beginning a new momentum, an excitement accompanied by the strongly felt sense that something needs to be done . . . (but soon this is blunted in recognition of) immense staff and organizational difficulties, increasing demands (and) great structural problems.[9]

Effective parish planning, then, is not for the faint of heart or the one night stand crusader!

THE LARGER DIMENSION

The focus here is parochial. But each parish, particularly in an hierarchic Church, swims in a diocesan sea. Likewise, each parish is a corporate citizen of a civic community. Thus, more or less overt in these pages, three larger dimensions must be recognized and then effectively factored into parish *planagement:*

a. *Region.* In all dioceses, proximate parishes are gathered in deaneries, area vicariates, now often in "clusters." Regional opportunities and imperatives impact increasingly on the local Church as clergy numbers decline and expectations multiply:

> In the future, it will be important that clusters of parishes work together so they can provide a wide spectrum of ministries and programs which are expected of good parishes today. Through such planning and collaboration, they can offer a number of quality educational, formational and social services which might be more than a single parish can provide. Indeed such collaboration is already occurring.[10]

There are many guidelines for the regional Church. By and large, though, it often fumbles and stumbles as it falls victim to parochial "islandism." It is, in fact, often ineffectual both as a vehicle and instrument for operations and for shared responsibility. I elaborate somewhat on this aspect of the regional Church in the chapter titled REDISCOVERY 4: CONTEXT. For the rest, I suggest that as parishes rediscover themselves and plan more wisely, more and more they will recognize the urgency for joint resourcing and action. This is also true of regionalism in its ecumenical dimension.

b. *Diocese.* A diocese should be a model and advocate for better sharing and planning not only in its chancery but also in all of its parishes. It convenes parochial leaders. It is a source of guidance, information, and inspiration. Local tentatives are reported, cumulated, and evaluated. Many dioceses have at least paraprofessional council and/or planning offices. This connection surfaces here and there below, particularly in the chapter titled REDISCOVERY 4: CONTEXT.

c. *Civics.* Parishes benefit from and should contribute to the civic commonwealths in which they subsist. For further comment, again, see the chapter titled REDISCOVERY 4: CONTEXT.

THE "MARKET" ANALOGY

Defining the customer is a top management priority.[11]

Often in these pages I use a "market" analogy. I refer to competition, to customers. A priest who read this text before it was finalized objected. Parishes, he argued, do not peddle a product. Their congregants and those they propose to influence are not customers. Everyone in a People of God Church is a principal. No one is an outsider, a spectator, merely a recipient. The analogy is inept!

Admittedly, we do not sell a tangible commodity like soap or cereal. Admittedly, we propose to involve more and more persons in ownership of our parishes rather than only as observers. Admittedly, the comparison, as all comparisons, limps. But parishes do compete for the presence and allegiance of people. It is never simply a matter of preaching and praying. Parishes too are immersed in "the human condition." Those we hope to engage are free spirits in a market in which there are many contesting forces. They can and do "shop around." They can and do buy and bet in a whole host of places. We need to canvas them. We need to magnetize them. I am reminded of what was reputed to be a Japanese sales practice before World War II. A Japanese company wishing to promote its products in a foreign location sent cameras and tapes to that location and recorded its public habits. Then they adjusted their products and their pitch to meet what they found. I do not suggest that we tailor our teachings to every current whim and fancy. I do suggest that this sort of canvas and response, this market analysis, is urgent for us too!

It is also evident that in every parish there are a few who serve and many who are served. True, the task is always to move more and more people from served to serving. Still, in the meanwhile, most Catholics and, surely, those we propose to influence, can legitimately be likened to customers.

It is, in any case, not idly that all current *planagement* texts stress the urgency for a customer orientation; nor that speaking to one discipline for moving action through "the human condition,"—cybernetics—one alert priest nearly two decades ago wrote: "even for the Church, the problems of a cybernetic age need cybernetic solutions."[12] Imperfect though it is, the market analogy provides us with a useful basis for reflection on how we share and plan in a very competitive and highly sophisticated market place!

TOMORROW?

Inescapably, my view of tomorrow threads through how I recommend parishes do their todays. There are currently in both Church and state prophets of doom and gloom. Some propose that "the end times" are near. Some contend that, unless certain ecclesial policies and polities change, we are headed for disaster. There are also optimists—like the Naisbitts. In every century, they remind us, there have been crises which have been perceived as catastrophic. Again and again the current doomsayers were proven wrong. We have always somehow survived. One American Cardinal is positive about tomorrow:

> The golden age is now. . . . I am confident that the best time for the Chicago parish and its priests is yet to come.[13]

Another is likewise positive:

> (Some say) that the Church is in a season of autumn. I firmly believe that we stand at the threshold of a season of springtime and new hope for the Archdiocese.[14]

Still another hierarch proclaims a "season of seeds":

> Planting seeds is about the future and the virtue of hope. . . . There will be pain . . . and a sense of loss. . . . We know that suffering, dying and death are a prelude to the experience of resurrection.[15]

Others preach a hopeful "patience."

I find myself somewhere in the middle. I am no Mary Poppins. I am no Cassandra. More and more I resonate the words of that outstanding world critic, Gunnar Myrdal. Speaking to us at an American Institute of Planners convention twenty-five years ago, he said:

> My experience in life as a social scientist and a social reformer has taken me far away from the simple trust in an easy and rapid advance through planning toward Eutopia, which was my spiritual heritage. I stick to the Ideals from enlightenment as firmly as ever. But I am less hopeful about their early realization or even about the feasibility of an approach to it. . . . I have been a planner all my life and will remain so. But I have increasingly been impressed by the staggering obstacles to overcome. . . . What the world needs now is not illusory optimism but the courage of almost desperation.[16]

I stand foursquare with Myrdal! Its pastors and its planners best practice the parish Church today with invincible optimism disciplined and muscled with the courage of almost desperation!!

[1] Joe B. Wyatt on his installation at Vanderbilt University, Nashville, February 24, 1983, reported in *The Vanderbilt Register*, (February 25, 1983) 5.

[2] Joseph Fichter S.J., to a Harvard Divinity School colloquium on "Churches and Synagogues in Boston Renewal," Cambridge, Mass., January 10, 1964.

[3] *Steeples in Metropolis* (Dayton, Ohio: Pflaum, 1969) 13, 14.

[4] Peter F. Drucker, *Managing the Future* (New York: Talley/Dutton, 1992) 228.

[5] Mark Fisher, "Parish Pastoral Councils: Purpose, Consultation, Leadership," National Pastoral Life Center (Paper #4), New York City, 1990, 1.

[6] "Model of the Church in Ministry," Center for Parish Development, Naperville, Illinois, 1979, 22.

[7] Ibid., 31.

[8] "Five Year Vision," Archdiocese of Minneapolis/St. Paul, 1981, 2.

[9] Robert R. Newsome, *The Ministering Parish* (New York: Paulist Press, 1982) 8.

[10] Joseph Cardinal Bernardin cited in *Origins* (1992) 787.

[11] Imai Masaaki, *Kaizen* (New York: Random House, 1986) 53.

[12] Patrick Granfield, *Ecclesial Cybernetics* (New York: MacMillan, 1963) xii.

[13] Bernardin, *Origins*, 784, 785.

[14] Edmund Cardinal Szoka, "Dying and Rising Together in Christ," Archdiocese of Detroit, 1989, 33.

[15] Archbishop Daniel W. Kucera O.S.B., letter in *The Witness*, Dubuque, Iowa, April 12, 1992.

[16] Washington D.C., October 3, 1967.

CHAPTER TWO

THE QUANTITY IMPERATIVE

> Involving individuals in the business is the most effective
> way to produce an organization in which people know more,
> care more and do the right things.[1]

Even the best parish council is few in numbers. The tendency in the contemporary Church to get things done rather through small groups than in plenary, grass roots sessions is understandable. And yet, for parishes as for all institutions, there is also what I call a quantity imperative. "Wholesale involvement yields wholesale success."[2] Not that we should stop nurturing councils and other parochial committees. They do need guidance and inspiration to grow in grace and wisdom. But we must go farther than merely this!

Several factors combine to support the quantity imperative. For instance, lay ministries multiply:

> It is indeed encouraging to note how lay people in ever-increasing numbers have become involved in the life of the Church in the United States and how this has led to a "depth and variety of ministry far greater than ever before." Certainly . . . this is an eloquent sign of the fruitfulness of the Second Vatican Council, one for which we all give thanks.[3]

Ministry is, however, in its broader sense more than the practice of a few designated individuals. Ministry is also parish councils and the people who sit in plain pews in every parish. Clearly, there is a need to activate them as well as staff persons. "When two or three people are involved, coordination and/or organization is necessary."[4] One goal in this kind of development is to extend continually the quantity of persons involved in being and doing parish. Where, on the other hand, such persons "have no commitment to a plan, a decision or a goal which they had no opportunity to influence,"[5] a WE versus THEY dysfunction happens.

While this chapter focuses primarily on numbers, the quantity imperative encompasses also measurability. A parish must become an ever wider WE numerically. It must also somehow quantify its plans and planlets* so that it can evaluate its progress in accomplishing them. It was not, for instance, surprising that Management by Objectives soon became Management by Objectives/Results. PROCESS and PAPERS can, in fact, so overwhelm any planning effort that it becomes inconsequential. Thus, in reflecting here on numerical quantity, we must also reflect on measurement.

People "will no longer accept decisions (which are) handed down to them."[6] A recent set of council guidelines says the same thing—"every effort must be made to involve parishioners in the decisions that affect their own growth."[7] The basic concern in all of this is ownership. Ownership is not something which can be decreed. It cannot occur when people are kept at a distance from moments and points at which owning decisions are taken. Ownership requires tangible involvement and an overt personal commitment. I still believe that most American Catholics want to be part of the dialogue as to the future of their parishes. But this will not be activated unless we somehow invite and involve them:

> When people are interested enough to come to the field, it would be unfair to confront them with closed hangar doors.[8]

---

*I use the term planlets to designate particular plans developed to implement an organization's general plan.

Parish councils impact on parochial tomorrows. To close the doors around them, limiting participation to their inevitable fewness, is a mistake. Sharing, therefore, confronts a continual quantity imperative.

> To be successful . . . vision and goals must grow out of the needs of the entire parish and be claimed and worked on by all.[9]

But if the rationale is obvious, the practice is difficult. An example from recent civics: In the course of "urban renewal," and the "War On Poverty," the concept of "citizen participation" emerged. It was variously phrased, e.g., "planning with, not just for, people." The idea was to dialogue urban change before it happened with those who would most immediately be impacted by it. Pat Moynihan called it "Maximum Feasible Participation." In the event, however, such "participation" frequently floundered. True, people do turn out to say no. They will come in crowds to oppose nearby developments which they dislike. They did not and they do not rally behind causes which are positive in even remotely comparable numbers. This kind of problem has been described as NIMBY (Not In My Backyard). I call it the asphalt factor! It was generally agreed in a Massachusetts city that a public asphalt plant was needed now. But when specific sites were proposed, massive neighborhood opposition emerged. So, too, in the Church. Call a meeting on how to improve this parish and few respond. Suggest specific changes, e.g., in sanctuary furnishings, in Mass schedules and many respond, but usually to oppose them.

Such considerations may seem to suggest that the likelihood for mounting positive numbers in accommodating the quantity imperative in a parish is slim. This is not my intent. It is my intent at the outset to emphasize that there will be many difficulties en route. At the risk of shortchanging a very big subject, several realities are involved here:

1. *Cynicism:* Already a decade ago, disillusionment with our institutions was evident:

The term "institution" is synonymous with failure to be attentive, influenced and responsive to the needs and insights of those it claims to serve.[10]

More recently, cynicism is even more rampant:

To be cynical about corporate motives is now normal, even chic. . . . (There is) a permeating lack of trust in society and in the future.[11]

Cynicism is fed from many sources. It extends far beyond the recent rebellion against "Beltway insiders." It is fueled by "anxiety, anomie and envy."[12] It is also fueled by what is perceived as sleight of hand on the part of institutional authority, "an element of smoke and mirrors in today's corporate revivalism."[13] They talk big, they promise much, but nothing really changes. *Plus ça change, plus c'est la même chose* (the more things seem to change, the more they remain the same). Not surprisingly, a similar sort of cynicism, and for many of the same reasons, afflicts the institutional Church.

2. *Dissent.* Polls again and again indicate that many Catholics dissent in their thinking and practice from ecclesial "teaching." Thus, a perennial quandary confronts us when we propose widely to involve these Catholics in advisory groups and events. On the one hand, Christ was a "sign of contradiction." The Church in its dioceses and parishes is similarly signed. It can never simply canvas what Catholics do and then throw holy water on it. It must proclaim a constant gospel, however much some details in that gospel may run counter to the practices of its members. On the other hand, by opposing what seem to be majority Catholic practices, it becomes increasingly hard to summon these same people to "participate." The fact that the kind of parochial sharing to which this text is directed is fenced off from dialogue on dissent categories in the Church Universal cannot alter the psychological resistance it will encounter from Catho-

lics whose lives are studded with dissent from official "teaching."

3. *Sophistication.* We are no longer the church of our ancestors with its relatively docile and uneducated pews. In most places we are no longer—though there are important immigrant pockets still—"new Americans" or even their sons and daughters. The challenge to share must work itself out in parishes with many sophisticates and much learning in our pews:

> Never in history have there been so many reasonably well-educated people, collectively armed with so incredible a range of knowledge. Never have so many enjoyed so high a level of affluence, precarious perhaps, but ample.[14]

And yet, in a judgment which is surely replicable below the border,

> Canadians with the highest incomes and the best education are the least interested in religion.[15]

There now sit in our pews, to put it another way, many movers and many shakers. But many no longer sit there, and many of those who still do are not otherwise "participating." Perhaps, indeed, "cynicism" is greater the wiser one is. Certainly, affluent and educated people will not be attracted by processes and structures which do nothing substantial! Likewise, movers and shakers are more familiar with the "smoke and mirror" problem in much of today's "corporate revivalism." When even the suspicion of this arises in parish advisory efforts, they will be quickly turned off. Another aspect to the sophistication factor is how best to mix these movers and shakers with the plain folk in a common dialogic process. Each has differing competences and differing expectations. Much skill is required to hold them both in any effective effort.

4. *The death of utopia.* After World War II, the scent of PROGRESS was heavy in the air we Americans breathed.

We were the undisputed arbiters, the champions of the Free World. Disillusionment has since set in. We are well into an Age of Austerity. We pull in our belts. Most of us no longer believe tomorrow will be drastically better than today. So too, whatever dreams we may have had about a magnificently better Church by the year 2000, they have long since ended in a much dimmer dawn. Indeed, the future is now clouded with uncertainties, many of them malevolent. "You must," said one business executive, "drive slower and know how to shorten your planning horizons when the fog index rises."[16] There are no utopias any more. There is, in both state and Church, much fog. Our contemporary task, therefore, becomes one of thinking shorter and expecting less. The net result has been twofold. We talk now of "chunking," breaking down giant goals into small, manageable pieces. We don't talk of "master plans." We move slowly step by step rather than proclaiming some systemic nirvana and then racing toward it with all out drums! And, unlike the philosopher kings of classic times, we increasingly recognize that we do not possess all at once that total truth of which heroic visions can be soon built. Indeed, a British priest suggested recently that

> Rather than unfolding by grand design, truth comes out slowly, piecemeal and grubby with all manner of fingerprints on it.[17]

But this sort of gradualism runs headlong into a wisdom enunciated a century ago by the architect of the Chicago Columbia Exposition, Daniel H. Burnham: "Make no little plans," he warned, "they have nothing in them to stir men's blood." It is much harder to stimulate and sustain enthusiasm for small steps than it is for eloquent marches toward some magnificent horizon. We need to recognize this difficult truth and deal with it. It is not ever a matter of abandoning the initial dream in HIM who is always our strength. It is always a matter of moving from the dream event down quickly into incremental actions. In the process, the divine fires of that dream must be kept bravely burning. Thus, the death of utopia—not certainly the utopias proposed in a "kingdom not of this world," but certainly the prospects of a swift and comprehensive establishment of this kingdom on earth—requires a new kind of patience, much seemingly minimal plodding, and shorter horizons as we implement wholesale parish participation in our planning. Here too major skills are required.

5. *Expectations.* And yet, we continue to want more and more from our institutions. We are well into the revolution of instant expectations! Even in the midst of "a steep rise in all the behavioral symptoms of increased anxiety"[18]—perhaps because of this—we demand more and more from our institutions, and we want service now:

> The "entitled" generation has limited capacity to delay its gratifications and no desire to sacrifice for the next generation.[19]

What have you done for me lately? A similar proliferation of instant expectations impacts on any parish which proposes to share and to plan better:

> (Priests widely testify to the fact that the) expectations of their people have risen dramatically in the last ten or fifteen years. The unrealistic and even contrary expectations of people and bishops have created standards that pastors try as they might could not always live up to completely.[20]

This combination of the search for immediate gratifications in a society in which utopia is dead yet "unrealistic" expectations abound raises many problems. It is compounded when an institution like a parish apparently only somehow and slowly responds. It is compounded too in a "counter-culture" Church.

6. *Diversity.* Diversity in a parish is a source of strength. It is also a source of many problems. In ethnically and ideologically homogenous communities, consensus is relatively easy. In many parishes yesterday, there was neither a need nor a capacity for pluralism. As we experience massively diverse parochial constituencies, the situation is much altered. True, we can approach such diversities with a Bismarckian wisdom. At international conferences, Bismarck said, I don't really care why this nation or that nation wants a certain outcome. All that matters to me is how their position affects my Imperial Germany. But parishes are not Reichs. Besides, with the death of utopia, there is usually no total and agreed leadership vision of what this parish should be. "Quality," in any case, "must be judged as the customer perceives it."[21] In a sense, parishioners are the customers of every parish (see pages 19, 20). We must know how they feel to serve them best. Market analysis is one way to say this. I suggest a parallel also from architecture. The architect constructs a three-dimensional model. Before he finalizes it, he stoops down and looks through that model from the street level. How will it be experienced by those who will inhabit it? So too, before finalizing any program, pastors, staff, and councils alike should stoop down often, look, and listen. How will those this program is designed to serve perceive it? In so doing they will, again, encounter much diversity. But at least they will now know this diversity in detail. And they can adjust the content and methodology of the program so far as possible to accommodate pluralism. There is, in short, no substitute for many canvasses at the pew level:

> We need always a thorough knowledge of the playing field, of our backyard and their backyards.[22]

Put another way, church leaders too must "keep looking for the different mirrors that others use to perceive reality."[23] Just by observing, obviously, we will not overcome diversity. There will be contention still between "progressives" and "traditionalists," between small community advocates and mega parish advocates. "Conflict resolution" becomes an integral element in parochial leadership. There are, besides, many ways and many words in parish planning:

> (There is) a plurality of effective models of organization for mission and ministry in parishes. . . . No one model has been canonized as the best model.[24]

In terms of its existential diversities, one model may work better in one parish, another in another. I cannot solve the problems of pluralism on the parochial level. I do suggest that (a) through spiritual discernment, and (b) through canvassing and understanding the viewpoints of the several diversities, pluralisms can at least begin to be harnessed in a workable, if not always placid, commonwealth. But the task, as we city planners found when we launched "citizen participation," will be neither easy nor quick!

If these are some of the pitfalls, what action is indicated? There is no panacea. One fact is compelling: If we really want to enable an ever WIDER parish WE, we must never elevate membership on some particular standing committee to where it becomes the exclusive criterion of participation in that parish. Most Americans will simply not accept membership of what I describe as *eternal committees.* * Perhaps they should, but they won't! To activate a numerical quantity imperative in a parish, opportunities to share must be widened beyond one or another eternal committee. Frequent canvasses and surveys are one way to do this. There are two other ways:

---

*Eternal committees meet forever, e.g., on the third Thursday evening of every work month.

1. *Task forces.* These are ad hoc groups gathered for a limited time to accomplish a given task in a given manner and to report back by a given date. Task forces exemplify what the *excellence* books refer to as "chunking." I do not mean in any way to denigrate those who serve on standing committees or to suggest we do not need such continuity. I do propose that by inviting them to specific sharing on a specific item in a specific timeframe, we will engage the graces and talents of far more parishioners than if we only summon them to an eternal committee. Besides, while standing groups survive often with no clear accomplishments, task forces can produce visible outcomes. There is a feeling of having done something useful. There is also the factor of new leadership. Quite possibly, engaged initially on a quick task force, new leaders may emerge for the longer haul!

2. *Assembly.* A parish assembly is an annual gathering of the entire parish to reflect on its "mission" and its "business." It too seeks to involve parishioners who simply will not rally to eternal committees or to continuous programs. A good assembly furthers the quantity imperative in these ways:

   a. It offers pastoral leaders a chance and a challenge to dialogue their visions and actualities with a large grass-roots congregation;
   b. It spotlights parish councils as bodies of substance with open ears in this parish;
   c. It provides an opportunity for diocesan and regional agencies and programs to engage in dialogue with their customers;
   d. It surfaces felt needs and concerns and it may also surface new leadership persons;
   e. It celebrates in liturgy and spiritual discernment the unity of this People of God with its pastor, and vice versa;

f. It can be the occasion for a keynote address and other talks which serve to reenlighten the entire parish;

g. It can be the occasion for reporting survey results and for polling those present on current and prospective parochial tentatives.

The practice of assemblies is already of long standing in American Protestant churches. It makes great sense. If an assembly will never engage the totality of any parish, still it will bring together in one long and constructive day many more people than will ever attend even the most effectively promoted "open meeting" of a parish council!

Two further factors impact on the quantity imperative as numbers. One is the fact and habit of *inertia*. René Dubos, the environmentalist, spoke often of the amazing tolerance of humankind. This is good in some instances, he conceded. But it has a negative side. We tend to relax in the face of "cosmic insults" until they have grown so big they are almost unmanageable. Even Dr. Russell Kirk, apostle of American conservatism, laments "a tendency to tolerate present imperfection in fear of radical and unknown alternatives."[25]

The *excellence* books and similar others repeatedly headline the importance of the habit of breaking the habits which constrain organizational initiative:

> Nothing less than a fundamental restructuring of traditional management systems will work. . . . REAL restructuring is an ongoing process not an event.[26]

There is also the "boiled frog" syndrome. Put a frog in cold water, then gently step up the heat. As the temperature rises, the frog adjusts. In the end, relaxing in the conviction that things will work out, he is boiled to death! And yet, wallowing in samenesses is easier and pleasant:

> Familiar routines are comforting and reassuring while abandoning or restructuring institutionalized behavior can be disquieting.[27]

It's not broken, why fix it? It's too simple to assume that everything is fine despite a few pin pricks. Too simple to canonize, like Tevye's "Tradition!" Inertia likewise saps the energies in many churches:

> Because the church is victimized by the gods of (static) goodness, it cannot deploy (its) power and resources where they can bring purpose and life to a vacillating world.[28]

Thus, seeking to involve more and more parishioners in an ever WIDER parochial WE, we confront a basic tug between the ease of inertia and the challenge to grow. Witness a recent comment about American archbishops:

> Planning has been ineffective in most archdioceses because planning means making choices and choices bring conflict with those who prefer the status quo.[29]

The second factor impacting on the quantity imperative in a parish is the so-called *advisory/decisive dilemma.* Advisory committees propose, pastors and staffs dispose. And this is as it must be in an hierarchic Church. Problems, however, arise in two dimensions. First, *near democracy:* The movement to a People of God polity encompassing many of the appearances of the "democracy" we Americans practice in our civic lives. We meet, we deliberate, we recommend, sometimes we vote. We come close to what we do in civics, but we never fully arrive. Thus we have a "near thing." Near things, like 3.2 percent beer and ersatz substitutions in wartime, never satisfy. We are tantalized by many statements to the effect that we too are Church, not just those who wear Roman collars. We are given data, we are convened. Meanwhile, despite repeated papal warnings, lines of distinction between clergy and laity blur. In these circumstances, people feel put down when they are told "you are only advisory, I decide around here." This hierarchic fact need not and should not be communicated in such a way, but often it seems to be. Second, *substance and results:* Every American was born in Missouri. We are a show-me people. We expect something to happen after we meet. If in councils or committees we convene and recommend and then nothing is done, we resent it. We feel frustrated. We feel we have wasted our time. Some of us may even abscond from sharing in the conviction that "Father will do what he wants anyhow." We will, in short, no longer meet to meet. We will meet only when there is meat on the gathering table or, at least, the prospect of meat soon afterward.

There is a way to defuse this dilemma. I call it a *democracy of means.* By this I mean that a pastor, after appropriate consultation, decides and proclaims an end (a goal). Within the twin constraints of feasibility and orthodoxy, parish staff and advisors then decide the best means (objectives) for accomplishing this goal. Such a process recognizes contemporary management theory:

> Planning for a future is not making a blueprint for absolute adherence. It is choosing a direction.[30]

Some prefer to call this the solution space method:

> The manager's job is to establish the boundaries around a fairly broad solution space. The individual's responsibility is to find the best way of doing things within that space.[31]

"Solution space" is no "blueprint." "Solution space" theory rather suggests courses of action in a given area of pastoral concern. It then challenges relevant individuals and groups to fill in that space with effective detail. For parochial deciders to lay on parochial advisors specific proposals in which every *i* is dotted and every *t* is crossed is counterproductive. Rather, let them propose "directions" and indicate parameters for action, then step back, allowing advisors to propose action detail and staff to do that detail. In this way, a new motivational energy sweeps through councils:

> People cannot be truly motivated by anyone else. . . . That door is locked from the inside; they should work in an at-

mosphere that fosters self-motivation . . . self-assessment
. . . and self-confidence.[32]

More than thirty years ago, Douglas MacGregor, in his *The Human Side of Enterprise*, proposed a Theory Y in management. The average American, he argued, is hardworking, responds to challenge, and must be affirmed in his or her responsibilities. He or she does this best in an atmosphere of respect and encouragement. So too in the "solution space" theory, doers and advisors in a parish are affirmed in their respective roles and accoladed as they perform:

> In directed autonomy people in every nook and cranny of the company are empowered, encouraged in fact, to do things their way. People know what the boundaries are.[33]

I submit that a parish which practices this kind of democracy of means is a parish in which the advisory-decisive obstacle to the quantity imperative is notably lessened.

Since the matter is so important, here more specifically is how a parish should implement its democracy of means:

1. Pastor with council consensus proclaims a parochial goal; for instance, to double the number of high school young persons regularly enrolled in our religious education program.

2. How to accomplish such a goal becomes the responsibility of relevant persons and committees within the parish. For instance, they may decide to begin by canvassing the current situation, asking questions of faculty and students. They may want to ponder available resources for beefing up content and numbers in their current program. They may review various methods and approaches. They specify one year objectives toward this three-year goal. They decide the details.

3. Pastor and staff may, of course, intervene at any point with suggestions. But the decision rests with the persons or committees involved. Two conditions are important:

3.1 Proposed actions and resource commitments must fall within the current or anticipated capacity of the parish;

3.2 Proposed actions must be consonant with diocesan and larger ecclesial directives in the subject area.

4. Thus the graces and talents of the advisory groups are fully martialled and respected. At the same time, having proclaimed the goal, the decisive prerogative of the pastor is sustained.

It seems obvious that as they become more substantive and consequential, parish councils operating in a democracy of means like this will become more and more attractive to more and more parishioners!

Quantity, again, is both numbers and *measurement*. This latter item is always proposed as a significant part of any *planagement* method.

> Measurement is the heart of any improvement system. If something cannot be measured, it cannot be improved.[34]

Measurement is indispensable:

> Measurement is the pivotal management and improvement tool. . . . Without measurement, management is a series of uneducated guesses. . . . Without measurement, one cannot specifically identify, describe and set priorities on problems.[35]

A recent diocesan task force agrees—(there should be) "some way to measure the effectiveness of parishes."[36] And yet this poses problems. Observing archbishops, one critic suggests:

> There are few empirical ways of measuring whether a (church) program is effective or not.[37]

I served once as vice president in a firm headed by a man who was one of the most prominent and earliest consultants with planning dioceses. Dr. Felix M. Lopez sought to bring to bear on sacerdotal accountability his long expertise in personnel evaluation. He ran into dissent. When he talked of holding priests accountable, one of them immediately responded, "but how do you quantify the priesthood?" How, for instance, do you measure "spirituality?" He conceded the difficulty. It is urgent, he argued, that to hold a priest accountable one must somehow quantify even such intangibles as "spirituality"; for instance, by keeping track of how many pious books he reads each month, his visits to the Blessed Sacrament, preparation and thanksgiving time at daily Mass, etc. Taken together, such indicators add up to a measurable factor. This can never penetrate the priestly heart and soul totally. It can provide a base for judgment and reform. Otherwise, as a priest proposes to improve his performance, he wrestles with imponderables and vagueness. I agree there is always the danger of strait-jacketing a quality in a quantity. A well-publicized pastor asks:

> How do we escape flat minded measurement? The gospel is so upside down to all human business measurements. . . . What organizational model fits the servanthood-leader model?[38]

But he adds quickly:

> Without evaluation, accountability and the like, it is easy for the ordained or nonordained minister to slip into individualism and idiosyncracy.[39]

Yet he appends a caution with which I totally resonate:

> Still a mighty discernment is needed lest we strike down the teacher and so modify the behavior of the prophet that we mute the voice we desperately need to hear.[40]

I come back as I started to certain fundamental truths. If their application to priests, dioceses, and parishes requires much skill, still they remain basic:

> While it is true that effects cannot always be weighed in ounces or grams or measured in inches and feet, the effects of any human endeavor can be ascertained in some mea-

sure, often by making glaringly obvious any discrepancy between purpose and declared objective.[41]

And again:

Accountability is a necessary part of all ministry and service. Ongoing personal and continual evaluation is necessary for continued growth.[42]

SUMMATION

There are two basic realities in which the quantity imperative in parochial sharing and planning locates. The first of these is the urgency for involvement of more and more parishioners throughout in ownership of the parish as an ever WIDER WE. The second of these is the urgency for so stating and evaluating parish goals and objectives as to permit their measurement both in progress and at term. The first is, thus, numerical, the second a matter of enunciation and follow through. Each of these is critical. Without them, on the one hand, a parish becomes, whatever its pretense, a kind of oligarchy, a *we* versus *they* situation. On the other hand, a parish could get lost in pious platitudes, drifting along, never sure if it is in point of fact accomplishing anything. I readily admit that this sort of tangibility runs counter to the position that religion simply can never be properly quantified. Still, despite all our divine adjacencies we remain human. If the wind in our collective sails cannot be meted and bounded, the energies in our oars and shoulders always can and must be assessed and converged.

[1] Edward E. Lawlor III, *The Ultimate Advantage* (San Francisco: Jossey-Bass, 1992) 347.

[2] Tom Peters, *Thriving on Chaos* (New York: Knopf, 1987) 214.

[3] Pope John Paul II, September 16, 1987.

[4] George M. Williams, *Improving Parish Management* (Mystic, Conn.: Twenty-Third Publications, 1983) 19.

[5] Arthur C. Beck, Jr., *Effective Decision Making for Parish Leaders* (Mystic, Conn.: Twenty-Third Publications, 1973) 12.

[6] Ibid.

[7] "Parish Pastoral Councils: Vision and Goals," Diocese of Joliet, Illinois, September 1990, 9.

[8] Charles A. Lindbergh, *The Spirit of St. Louis* (New York: Scribner's, 1953) 15.

[9] "Parish Pastoral Councils," 19.

[10] Robert R. Newsome, *The Ministering Parish* (New York: Paulist Press, 1982) 3.

[11] Donald L. Kantner and Philip M. Marvis, *The Cynical Americans* (San Francisco: Jossey-Bass, 1989) 63.

[12] Ibid., 89.

[13] Ibid., 134.

[14] Alvin Toffler, *The Third Wave* (New York: Morrow, 1980) 455.

[15] Rae Correlli, *MacLean's Weekly* (Toronto, January 5, 1987) 58.

[16] Clifton Garvin, Chairman of the Board, Exxon; Vanderbilt University, Nashville, Tennessee, November 11, 1982.

[17] Michael Morton, *Priests and People* (London periodical, February 1992) 53.

[18] Yankelovich, *New Rules* (New York: Random House, 1981) 184.

[19] Kantner and Marvis, *The Cynical Americans*, 144.

[20] "A Shepherd's Care," NCCB/USCC, 19, 29.

[21] Tom Peters, *Thriving on Chaos*, 82.

[22] Thomas Morgan to a convention of the National Pastoral Planning Conference, Orlando, Florida, March 5, 1990.

[23] Robert H. Waterman, *The Renewal Factor* (New York: Bantam Books, 1987) 175.

[24] United States Catholic Conference, "Envisioning the Future of Mission and Ministries," *Origins* (November 9, 1989) 382.

[25] Nichols College lecture, Dudley, Massachusetts, November 18, 1981.

[26] C. Jackson Grayson and Carla O'Dell, *American Business: A Two-Minute Warning* (New York: Free Press, 1988) 119.

[27] Robert H. Schaeffer, "The Psychological Barriers to Management Effectiveness," *Business Horizons* (April 1971) 5.

[28] Bruce Blackie, *Gods of Goodness* (Philadelphia: Westminster Press, 1975) 168.

[29] Thomas Reese, S.J., *Archbishop* (New York: Harper and Row, 1989) 358.

[30] Williams, *Improving Parish Management*, 11.

[31] Waterman, *The Renewal Factor* (New York: Bantam Books, 1987) 1, 90.

[32] Tom Peters and Nancy Austin, *Passion for Excellence* (New York: Random House, 1985) 206.

[33] Waterman, *The Renewal Factor*, 75.

[34] IBM executive Harrington, cited in Peters, *Thriving on Chaos*, 74.

[35] Richard S. Sloma, *How to Measure Managerial Performance* (New York: MacMillan, 1980) 167.

[36] United States Catholic Conference, *Origins*, 383.

[37] Reese, *Archbishop*, 352.

[38] Rev. William Bausch, *Traditions, Tensions, Transitions in Ministry* (Mystic, Conn.: Twenty-third Publications, 1982) 105.

[39] Ibid.

[40] Ibid., 106.

[41] Newsome, *The Ministering Parish*, 92.

[42] Edmund Cardinal Szoka, *Dying and Rising Together With Christ* (Archdiocese of Detroit, 1989) 32.

CHAPTER THREE

THE RECKON ROAD

My logo has long since been *FROM INSIGHT TO IM-PACT.* I mean by this:

- a systematic and prayerful process through which
- a parish moves from new understandings about itself
- and its adjacencies
- through dialogue, consensus, and decision
- to a consequential parish plan
- which specifies roles, relationships,
- goals, and objectives
- in actionable detail.

The parish renews its insight and, if you will, its outsights. There are tangible results. The connection between "research" and outcome is throughout paramount. If on the other hand a parish simply meets and issues pious intentions, its planning and sharing cannot succeed. Likewise, if it moves too quickly and thoughtlessly into action, its planning and its sharing are fundamentally flawed. My approach is thus closed-ended. Architects can discuss houseness at length. But unless and until they build a house here and now for this client, they starve. Engineers can discuss roadness and bridgeness at length. But unless and until they build a road or a bridge here and now for this public client, they starve. A closed-end methodology requires decisions to include or to exclude at point after point in a deliberate movement from insight to impact. For instance, using the architectural analogy, see Illustration 3.1 on page 44.

Likewise, as a parish progresses from its insights and outsights to its preferred action impacts, it must at point after point:

- weigh alternatives
- select one, reject the others
- build forward item by item on the base of these previously selected options

This closed-end approach proposes, quite frankly, that whatever the ideal and the dream, a parish must progressively choose and plan accordingly as it moves from its "research" to its planned action. This closed-end approach emerges, as has been earlier indicated, from the design sciences. It is practical. It works. It forces planning parishes to recognize and accommodate throughout the *transfer factor:* how will we get this paper done with these people in this place here, now, and the day after tomorrow?

I have more recently coined a new acronym for my parish planning approach. I call it walking the RECKON ROAD. This, as detailed below, is a play on the first letters of each step in that approach. *R*ediscovery, *E*ngagement, *C*ommitment, then *K*eep *ON*. It further details but by no means replaces my fundamental logo—FROM INSIGHT TO IMPACT. Hopefully, it too is memorable!

I am well aware that other planning methodologies and semantics exist. I neither rate nor denigrate any of these. I do suggest that the system enunciated in these pages makes much sense, has been tested, and will work. I suggest also that any parish proposing to plan must from the start pick one method, one language, one schedule (MLS) and stick with it. To mix approaches is to risk a Tower of Babel in which everyone loses.

Following are two illustrations which introduce the RECKON ROAD.

Illustration 3.1

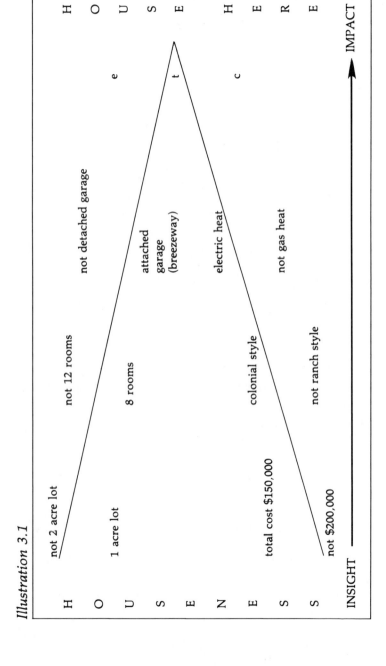

HOUSE HOUSE Het ec

IMPACT

not detached garage

attached garage (breezeway)

electric heat

not gas heat

not 12 rooms

8 rooms

colonial style

not ranch style

not 2 acre lot

1 acre lot

total cost $150,000

not $200,000

HOUSENESS

INSIGHT

Illustration 3.2

SHARING: ITINERARY ON THE RECKON ROAD

Rediscovery
1. The DREAM event, daring the dream, starting to do the dream in a good mission statement
2. The FACTS about ourselves
3. How we FEEL about ourselves
4. Our CONTEXT, how we benefit from and contribute to the larger ecclesial and civic communities of which we are a part

Engagement
5. Our LEADERS deliberate the data from Rediscovery, which is also widely distributed in the parish
6. Using the planning methodology we have selected, our leaders draft a mission statement, goals, objectives, relationships, etc., then consensus, and record them again for wide parish distribution

Commitment
7. As an ever WIDER WE, we gather in a series of open parish meetings
8. We review the data from Rediscovery and the drafts from Engagement
9. Facilitated and guided by our leaders, we deliberate the proposed mission statement, goals, objectives, and relationships to consensus
10. We then record key data and our approved goals and objectives in a parish pastoral plan
11. We commission this plan at a memorable liturgy and distribute it widely in the parish

K
e
e
p

O
N

We periodically evaluate our progress in plan implementation. We set sequential goals and objectives as may be appropriate. Thus, our plan is alive and again and again updated.

Through all of these steps, we recognize that unless the Spirit plans with us, we plan in vain! Our "common effort to attain fullness in unity" (*Documents of Vatican II*, "Dogmatic Constitution on the Church," 13) can succeed only if we are indeed a "Gospel people" experiencing a local Pentecost!

Illustration 3.3   Here is another way of looking at your parish as it begins to walk the RECKON ROAD:

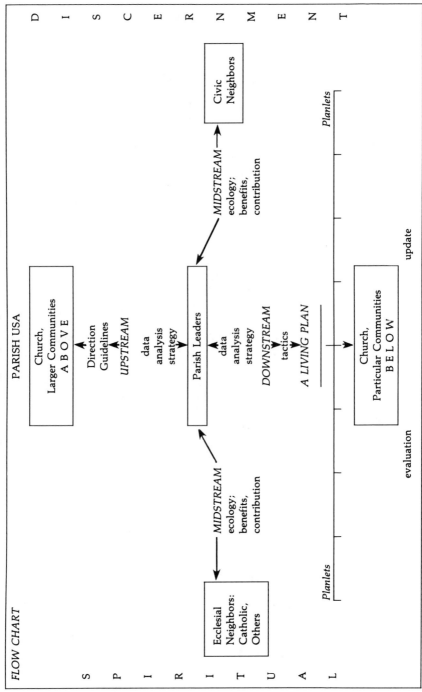

FLOW CHART

PARISH USA

S P I R I T U A L   **D I S C E R N M E N T**

Church,
Larger Communities
A B O V E

Ecclesial
Neighbors:
Catholic,
Others

↑ Direction
Guidelines
UPSTREAM

MIDSTREAM
ecology;
benefits,
contribution

data
analysis
strategy

Parish Leaders

MIDSTREAM
ecology; benefits,
contribution →

Civic
Neighbors

data
analysis
strategy

DOWNSTREAM
tactics

A LIVING PLAN

Church,
Particular Communities
B E L O W

Planlets

evaluation   update

Planlets

CHAPTER FOUR

DOWN THE RECKON ROAD:
Rediscovery

> If we could first know where we are and whither we are tending, we could then better judge what to do and how to do it.[1]

Our parish itinerary down the Reckon Road starts with REDISCOVERY. This can be otherwise described as a situation audit. It has many advantages:

> (A situation audit provides) a forum for sharing and debating divergent views about relevant changes. . . . (It helps) make vague opinions about certain different parts of the situation more explicit. . . . (It becomes) an intellectual exercise to stimulate creative thinking. . . . (It provides) a data base for completing strategic planning in all its phases.[2]

In a good REDISCOVERY process, the entire local People of God is canvassed and involved in four dimensions: dream, feelings, facts, context! Failure to probe and record data in any of these dimensions flaws any situation audit. Already in this initial stage of its planning effort, the parish reaches out to widen its ownership base:

> The greater the loyalty of the members of a group toward the group, the greater is the motivation among the members of the group to achieve the goals of the group, and the greater is the probability that the group will achieve its goals.[3]

CRITICAL PASTORAL CONCERN AREAS

As it seeks out data in its start-up situation audit, the parish at the same time enunciates a series of what are describable as critical pastoral concern areas and pigeonholes that data into these categories as far and as often as is appropriate. Critical pastoral concern areas (CPCAs) identify the range of mission/ministry with which an alert planning parish must reckon. Without such guidance and reference points, some major matter of pastoral accountability might be neglected. Critics and dioceses approach the CPCA matter differently. One recommendation called for eleven or more "other" issues ranging from "Pastoral Authority" through "Ministries of Care and Service" to "Parish Mission and Apostolic Community."[4] The Archdiocese of Baltimore in 1985 proposed seven, ranging from "Parish Worship" to "Parish Leadership and Management." The Archdiocese of Portland, Oregon, in its current "Parish Planning Document," enumerates four "areas of mission" ranging from "Ministry of the Word" to "Ministry of Service in and for the World" and adds five "areas of special concern" ranging from "Leadership Development" to "Community Outreach." There is no one best format, but the principle and the need remain compelling. Perhaps some kind of disjunction like this is appropriate:

a. Faith community
b. Faith formation
c. Family life (to comprehend marriage, youth, seniors, etc.)
d. Outreach (civil, ecclesial, service, peace and justice, etc.)
e. Administration (finance, buildings, staff, grounds)
f. Participation and planning (councils, assembly, plans, *planlets*).

In any case, I now strongly recommend that rather than being shoved subliminally into another category, planning and participation deserve and demand a specific category of their own in any listing of parochial CPCAs. I strongly recommend too that if and as a diocese summons its parishes to plan, it communicate one set of CPCAs so that there may be uniformity in reporting. Otherwise, here as elsewhere, it becomes increasingly hard for the diocese to advise its parishes and to cumulate canvass results.

PARISH INDICATORS

As a parish rediscovers itself, it surfaces what has come to be known as "parish indicators." These are the statistics and homegrown opinions which specify the state of this parish here and now. Canvassing itself thus in four dimensions, the parish responds to an obvious institutional "need for systematic approaches to (its) information requirements."[5] Parish indicators constitute "an important tool" and a "valuable means for improving the effectiveness of parish pastoral ministry."[6] They are also helpful for "self-measurement and for diocesan level use for evaluation and distribution of resources."[7] Parish indicators should be quantified so far as is feasible. They should be simply stated and easily understood, comprehensive, current, and focused on those factors which most significantly impact on the parochial community.

Dioceses have approached their parish situation audits via a series of parish indicators differently. Some have been long on objective data but strangely short on subjective data. Some use the terms "needs analysis." Many do not include either the dream category or the context category. All dioceses, however, do require parishes periodically to submit to the chancery certain sacramental, fiscal, and other local detail. If this is so, why a situation audit in the course of REDISCOVERY? The response is twofold:

1. True, much data does exist. But this is often piecemeal. Some information appears on one chancery form, some

on another, etc. Some is accurately current, other data is not. Besides, attitudinal canvasses are almost never reported to the diocese. And I know of no instance in which a thorough context canvass or the consequences of a good parochial dream event was reported to the diocese. Thus, while some information pertinent to a parish situation audit does indeed preexist in written form, much does not. In the course of REDISCOVERY, gaps are closed, figures rechecked for accuracy and comprehensiveness, and categories covered which to date have not been covered.

2. REDISCOVERY requires pastor, staff, and people together to seek out, analyze, and project forward from a very wide data base. All the information is collected at one time and surfaced in one clear and clean report. It has been checked carefully for accuracy, completeness, and currency. Thus, such a broad situation audit becomes a basic experience as well as a major initial necessity as a parish proposes better to share and to plan.

Action Steps

1. Check with your diocese to see if it has promulgated a list of critical pastoral concern areas (CPCAs). If it has, by all means use this list with no alterations. If not, develop your own list, seeking appropriate advice as you do so.

2. In each of the four phases in REDISCOVERY the kind of parish indicators which are required is carefully specified. Make certain each set of indicators is accurate, comprehensive, and current.

3. Suppose at the conclusion of your first steps down the RECKON ROAD in REDISCOVERY, you decide that responsive action in some CPCA is either not indicated or not feasible; in short, that you already do together as much as you can (or should) in this area! What then?

At least you will have surfaced and categorized all the indicators available to you in terms of that CPCA. You will have pondered this data. You will likewise have reexamined your response in and to it. Thus, even if no further action is required of you, you have deliberately reflected on one subject area in which parochial mission/ministry is urgent.

4. As each category in REDISCOVERY is completed, record what you have found simply and clearly. When all four categories have been completed, put everything together in staccato and digest format. Distribute this report throughout the parish. It will also, of course, constitute a basic resource as you and your leaders walk farther down the RECKON ROAD in ENGAGEMENT, COMMITMENT, and KEEP ON.

[1] Cited in George A. Steiner, *Strategic Planning* (New York: Free Press, 1979) 126.

[2] Ibid., 125, 126.

[3] Rensis Likert, *The Human Organization* (New York: McGraw Hill, 1967) 64.

[4] Robert R. Newsome, *The Ministering Parish* (New York: Paulist Press, 1982) 15.

[5] Published papers from a workshop at the National Pastoral Planning Conference convention in San Antonio, Texas, February 1979, 2.

[6] Ibid., 3.

[7] Ibid., 5.

CHAPTER FIVE

REDISCOVERY ONE: DREAM

Goals are dreams with deadlines and lifelines.[1]

REDISCOVERY encompasses a good deal of data gathering. But it begins best with the dialogue and daring of a dream. Dreaming, it has been aptly noted,

> is a game in a way, but a game with a purpose . . . (to spur) our creativity in an Age of Unreason.[2]

Dreams stretch "leaders into greater ability and creativity in their work."[3] One of the most effective "motivation(s) to change" occurs,

> if a leader can create a vision of a better world and provide strong support for such a vision.[4]

The evidence for reconceiving and repracticing our parishes is abundant. So is the need for innovative approaches. One critic calls these "upside down thinking—new ways of thinking about familiar things."[5] Daring a local dream is an excellent initial step toward upside down thinking in a parish! Scripture puts it this way:

> Without vision the people perish. (Proverbs 29:10)

Vision taps into idle energies. Normally, social scientists tell us we use only a small portion of our talents; likewise our graces! When we dream, not only do we set up ideals but we also challenge people to activate these deep personal resources. We see new opportunities:

> People don't get excited about jobs; they get excited about possibilities. Vision is the articulation of possibilities.[6]

Dag Hammarskold saw his task at the United Nations to be showing the nations where north is. Our north includes, surely, what Spirit and Book say to us. But there is also a need, further, to specify these basic norths in terms of the parochial here, now, and the days after tomorrow! Such a north becomes a principal reference point to which we relate and according to which we measure our programs.

Parochial dreaming is dialoguing, agreeing, and then stating a corporate vision. But the dream itself is only a start. Dreams alone are as inconsequential as hot air balloons. They soar above the terrain; they do not change it. Effective dreams require timeframes (deadlines); effective dreams require hands, feet, dollars, and voices (lifelines).

DARING THE DREAM

WHAT? A dream is a scenario of what its pastor and people would like this parish to be and become if it were released from such current gravities and fences as limited staff, limited monies, and limited horizons. A dream is, however, not a total utopia. Dreamers must avoid "the Camelot phenomenon."

The parochial dream process is initiated at an open meeting in which the question is posed, and dialogue ensues on these questions: What is a spiritually successful contemporary North American parish? How would you recognize and describe it?

WHY? The case for dreaming has already been made. Suffice it to clarify it further. Dreaming is "idealized design":

> (This) facilitates participation in the planning process. . . . (This is) usually fun. . . . (It) stimulates a cooperative atmosphere in which differences come to be treated as minor hurdles rather than as nonnegotiable conflicts. . . . (It generates) a commitment to realization of the idealized design. . . . (It) stimulates creativity and focuses it on organizational and individual development.[7]

Indeed, "the selection of ideals lies at the very core of interactive planning."[8] Beyond this basic wisdom there is another advantage in a dream event. When one "plans with people," it is always preferable to take them down a *yes* road as far as possible. There will be crossroads soon enough. There will be forks in the road soon enough, options and divergences. But if one, through idealized design, prolongs the journey down the *yes* road as far as may be feasible, the chances for commonwealth later increase. Consider: suppose, instead, a parish begins with canvasing its parishioners on the local level. Quickly, varying views contend. For instance, if you ask—What do you think of the music here? At once respondents divide and the music people bristle. Toes are stepped on. By daring a detached dream first, on the other hand, ideas emerge with no local baggage! Pastors and people walk unfettered down a *yes* road. Put another way, they develop together a blueprint of the house they would prefer to live in. There is a sense of convergence, of ownership, both of which are critical as they proceed beyond the dream to the deed.

WHEN?   Though both are intertwined, vision precedes mission. A parish probably should begin to gather local data even prior to daring its dream. But none of this should be communicated before the dream event. Nor should a parish write its mission statement before it has dreamed.

HOW?   An open parish meeting is announced and very strongly promoted. After appropriate prayer, the dreaming rationale, process, and expectation are carefully explained. The meeting moderator stresses that there is to be *no debate.* He or she then poses the two questions: What is a spiritually successful contemporary North American parish? How would you recognize and describe it? If an item is proposed from the floor, e.g., increasing lay ministries, the moderator simply asks, Does anyone disagree with this? If a hand is raised, he/she may suggest further clarification from the proposer(s). But *no argument.* A show-of-hands vote is then taken. If more hands go up in favor, the item is recorded on newsprint largely. If more hands go up opposed, the item is not recorded. Once the dream event has been completed, parish leaders may elect to announce the results of the recent attitudinal survey via written handouts. Indeed, such a procedure, with subsequent dialogue, makes considerable sense.

WHERE?   A comfortable place at a convenient time, announced well ahead, possibly in the course of the saturation weekend canvass—and very strongly promoted.

BEGINNING TO DO THE DREAM

"Dreams not desparation," says one critic, "move organizations to the highest level of performance."[9] But dreams alone are never enough. There must be both "viability and vision."[10] The parish has climbed an important peak, but it must not relax on the heights:

> There is always the temptation to proclaim just the dream and remain on the top of the mountain, contemplating its joy. If the parish succumbs to this temptation, the dream can't walk.[11]

Once the dream has been dared, the task is incarnational. If that dream is vision, how does it become mission? Scripture is apt:

> And the Lord said to me:
> write the vision,
> make it plain upon tablets
> so he may run who reads it.
>   (Habakkuk 2:2)

As it descends from the unincorporated euphoria of its dream, the parish develops a mission statement. This has been variously described, e.g.:

- "The group's reason for existence, its purpose and philosophy"[12]
- "(The identification of) fundamental commitments (and) a resource for management"[13]
- "(It) gives direction and meaning to all activities in the parish"[14]
- "(It) enunciates a purpose that integrates the variety of roles that a system plays."[15]

Mission statements in business are usually tilted toward bottom-line expectations. Mission statements in nonprofit institutions are often considerably less tangible.

A mission statement in a parish is the consensus proclamation by its pastor and people of the basic reasons why this parish exists here and now. It must be *local* to the parish, i.e., homegrown, not copied from some other parish. It must *inspire as well as inform.* It must be *spiritual.* It should, in my view—though the point is moot, be deliberately *concise,* e.g., not more than four or five sentences.[16] It need not and should not sprawl over everything from Genesis to Golgotha—and beyond! It must emerge from the *entire parish.* It should be initially drafted by parish leaders. But it must not be finally written and owned only by some blue-ribbon committee meeting jealously behind closed doors. Here, though it is considerably longer and broader than I would prefer, is an actual mission statement developed in 1990 in a large midwestern suburban parish with no school:

> _____ Parish is established to bring us together as a Catholic Faith Community. We will provide support for all our members through liturgy/worship/education, especially religious education/service/social events and the simple enjoyment of each other.
>
> We will be witnesses to the Christ Who has touched our lives. We will proclaim His Gospel and be His Church. We also recognize and support a responsibility to the larger community of the _____ area, the Diocese and the World. So the pursuit of justice is an important concern.
>
> Our parish life will center on the Eucharist during which we celebrate the presence of the Risen Lord among us. As a baptized faith community, we the people of _____ Parish will be filled with the Spirit of Jesus Who brings new life to us all.

Read this carefully. It is not atypical. It is hard if not impossible to conceive of any reasonable parish program which could not, in some way, be plugged into it! Thus, one conclusion is inescapable: mission statements, from an operational point of view, have little practical value!

Their importance, however, must not be minimized:

> Communion and mission are profoundly connected with
> each other. They interpenetrate and mutually imply each
> other to the point that communion represents source and
> the fruit of mission. Communion gives rise to mission and
> mission is accomplished in communion.[17]

Once a parish has dared its unincorporated dream, it must
begin its descent into reality. Its idealized design, its vision,
must be incarnated in a local mission statement. It must
reckon with its actualities and rediscover its purpose for existence. This is never a matter of simply throwing new holy
water on its inertias. Mission statements are immensely valuable at this planning stage for both spiritual and psychic
reasons. Consider: Catholics notoriously fail to "witness"
to each other. Seldom if ever are parishioners summoned
to convene with their pastors and ponder why they so convene. There is a healthy overtness in a mission statement
process which enables and requires communal witnessing.
Pastors and people sit together, pray together, then together
speak their deepest and highest thoughts as to the purpose
of the communities of faith, grace, and service in which they
assemble. This is a most "teachable moment!" At the same
time, pastors, staffs, and people are reminded of those taller
expectations which overarch their respective busynesses. Doing this, they rediscover a unity in prayer and purpose which
may have eluded them earlier. Mission statements, too, serve
as wonderfully appropriate texts for parish council retreats,
for days of recollection etc. While, then, a mission statement, and particularly in a nonprofit institution, is nonoper-
ational, it does set up high hopes and specify dedications
against which every so often parish doers and advisors alike
can measure themselves.

ACTION STEPS

1. When your parish leaders convene in ENGAGEMENT,
   explain and dialogue the logic, role, and significance of

a good mission statement. They will at this time have before them parish facts, feelings, and context gathered in the course of REDISCOVERY.

2. Ask them to reflect, pray, and seek consensus, and by a given date, create one or several possible mission statement draft(s).

3. Convene the parish as a whole. This at the first or second meeting in COMMITMENT. Review the proposed draft(s). If rewording is indicated, reedit. Choose among alternatives if several drafts emerge.

4. Incorporate the decided statement in your final parish plan and return to it often for refreshment and reinspiration.

[1] A sign on the electronic billboard in front of the Alexian Brothers Hospital in St. Louis, Missouri reads "Goals are dreams with deadlines." I expand it to read "Goals are dreams with deadlines and lifelines."

[2] Charles Handy, *The Age of Unreason* (Boston: Harvard Business School Press, 1981) 252.

[3] Arthur C. Beck, *Effective Decision Making for Parish Leaders* (Mystic, Connecticut: Twenty-Third Publications, 1973) 20.

[4] Edward E. Lawlor III, *The Ultimate Advantage* (San Francisco: Jossey-Bass, 1992) 341.

[5] Handy, *The Age of Unreason*, 24.

[6] James A. Behohla, *Championship Management* (Cambridge, Mass.: Productivity Press, 1990) 133.

[7] Russell L. Ackoff, *Creating the Corporate Future* (New York: Wiley and Sons, 1981) 116, 118, 119, 120.

[8] Ibid., 1.

[9] Robert H. Waterman, *The Renewal Factor* (New York: Bantam Books, 1987) 312.

[10] Robert R. Newsome, *The Ministering Parish* (New York: Paulist Press, 1982) 18.

[11] Ibid., 42.

[12] Beck, *Effective Decision Making*, 12.

[13] Joseph L. Imesch, "Parish Pastoral Council: Visions and Goals" (Diocese of Joliet, Ill., September, 1990) 9.

[14] Archdiocese of Baltimore, "Parish Planning and Administrative Manual," 1985, 37.

[15] Ackoff, *Creating the Corporate Future*, 107.

[16] In the Northwest Cascades Presbytery of Portland, it is advised that a mission statement should be "approximately 250 words in length," in "A Guide for Mission: Self-Study for the Local Church," Richard A. Miller, 1989, 44.

[17] John Paul II, "Christian Lay Faithful," #32 (Vatican City, 1988).

CHAPTER SIX

REDISCOVERY TWO: FACTS

The second dimension in REDISCOVERY is objective. What are the facts? What are the observable trends? What is the track record and what are the prospects of parish offices, programs, advisory groups?

There are, again, varying ways and words. In the mid-1980s the Archdiocese of Baltimore posed "two questions" on the "Parish Information Form." In the early 1990s the Archdiocese of Dubuque developed a nine page "Parish Self-Study Form." In the current Archdiocese of Portland "Parish Planning" document, five "planning forms" are appended. The first calls for civic community data, the second for parochial statistics. The third requests a list of parish pastoral programs; the fourth, optional, asks for further current and prospective details on particular programs. The fifth, also optional, proposes goal setting in each "Area of Mission."

In whatever format it occurs, objective REDISCOVERY requires some sort of instrumentation and process. Instruments must be so designed:

- As to surface accurate, complete, and current data
- As to collect in one place all pertinent data, e.g., fiscal reports, job descriptions, parish histories, group memories, and trends

- As to permit easy categorization into those critical pastoral concern areas which the parish has selected for itself
- As to avoid ambiguity and subjective tilting

Following are certain sample instruments. They are by no means proposed as absolute or necessarily best. They do respond to the above criteria.

When completed, returns from such instruments are carefully cumulated, reviewed, and then synopsized. It may be prudent to publish this synopsis at once. It may be preferable to wait until all four phases of REDISCOVERY have been accomplished and then to publish all the data at once. The latter approach is probably better. In any case, the facts data as all the data should be digested, univocally presented and, in time, made available to the parish as a whole and to parish leaders as they proceed down the RECKON ROAD in ENGAGEMENT!

Illustration 6.1

Parish: _____ Place: _____ Date: _____

COMMUNITY DEMOGRAPHY

Population	1980	1990*	% change
Total	_____	_____	_____
By Age:			
0–8	_____	_____	_____
9–17	_____	_____	_____
27–35	_____	_____	_____
45–53	_____	_____	_____
54–61	_____	_____	_____
61–65	_____	_____	_____
65+	_____	_____	_____

Ethnic Composition			
African American	_____	_____	_____
Asian/Pacific	_____	_____	_____
Hispanic	_____	_____	_____
Native American	_____	_____	_____
White	_____	_____	_____

Median Income	_____	_____	_____

This data should be available to parishes encompassing an entire community and through a combination of census tracts for parishes which encompass only parts of a single community, from state census offices and/or from metropolitan planning offices.

*If later figures are available, another column should be provided to date and record them.

(see also REDISCOVERY FOUR: CONTEXT, pp. 84–96)

Illustration 6.2

PARISH: BASIC DATA

	1980	1986	1988	1990	1991
Census Totals					
Mailing list	___	___	___	___	___
Regular Contributors	___	___	___	___	___
Sacramental					
Infant Baptisms	___	___	___	___	___
Adult Baptisms	___	___	___	___	___
First Communions	___	___	___	___	___
Confirmations	___	___	___	___	___
Weddings	___	___	___	___	___
Funerals	___	___	___	___	___
Catechesis					
Elementary					
# enrolled	___			___	___
% of total *	___			___	___
High School					
# enrolled	___			___	___
% of total *	___			___	___
Adult	___			___	___
School					
Parish students	___			___	___
Non-Parish students	___			___	___
Minority students	___			___	___

Weekend Services
Church capacity_____
Actual attendance weekend of_____: _____
Mass hours currently: Saturday_____Sunday_____
Individual Penance hours_____

Institutional Services
Hospitals served: #_____ # of beds:_____
Nursing homes served: #_____ # of beds:_____

* Of all those who should be enrolled in such catechesis, only a percentage are actually enrolled. Estimate this percentage.

Illustration 6.3

PARISH ADVISORY GROUPS

Name of Group_____Date established_____

Person Reporting_____ Office_____

Our **Mission** * _____

_____.

In the course of the past two years, these have been our principal **Accomplishments:**

In the course of the past two years, we have encountered these principal **Difficulties:**

In the course of the next three years, these are the principal things we hope to accomplish, our **Goals:**

To help us accomplish our goals and implement our Mission better, these are some **Things We Would Like To See Happen** in our parish:

ITEM   BY WHOM

Please add below any other comments which will further elucidate where and how this group now is and how it could become more effective, i.e., in performance and group satisfaction:

* Either as it has been overtly stated and communicated to the group or as the group now interprets it.

ONE SUCH FORM IS TO BE COMPLETED
BY EACH ADVISORY GROUP

Illustration 6.4

FINANCES*

Place in your objective data file a copy of your current budget and balance sheet.

Estimate overall parish expenses and receipts in the next three years. Place this projection in your objective data file.

CHARTERS OF ACCOUNTABILITY*
(Job Descriptions)

Place in your objective data file copies of the charters of accountability (job descriptions) of each full-time and part-time member of the parish staff.

Canvass the current service expectation and practice of any and all persons who contribute at least ten hours per week on an average as volunteer(s) to some parochial task. Place the results in your objective data file.

OTHER*

Place in your objective data file any other document which is relevant, e.g., a recent parochial history, a major school report, research in adult education in the parish, evaluations of particular programs, etc.

---

* Many if not all of the above materials may already exist in one form or another. The intention here is to gather them into one place so that any subsequent review of the facts about your parish can locate them easily and totally. In reporting this sort of data, obviously you will want to synopsize rather than merely duplicate.

Illustration 6.5

Parish:_____ Place:_____ Date:_____

CRITICAL PASTORAL CONCERN AREA (CPCA):*

_____

1. Outline briefly how your parish now responds to this CPCA. Summarize those programs which flesh out this response, indicating in each instance the number of the program as you report it in Illustration 6.6.

Response outline_____

_____

Programs (*see Illustration 6.6*)

2. Resource allocation in this Critical Pastoral Concern Area:

Resource	Sufficient	Needs Some Improvement	Needs Much Improvement
Staff: #_____	☐	☐	☐
Volunteers: #_____	☐	☐	☐
Dollars: $_____	☐	☐	☐
Facilities/Equipment:_____	☐	☐	☐

3. Dialogue and agree upon one good goal in this Critical Pastoral Concern Area. By and large, your goal should not merely reinforce inertia but rather deal with something you have above identified as needing some or much improvement.**

Goal Statement:_____

_____

This goal was developed by _____
    and agreed on _____
The accomplishment of this goal is the primary responsibility
    of_____
To accomplish this goal, we need these resources:
    a. People (staff and volunteers): _____
    b. Dollars: _____
    c. Facilities/Equipment, etc. _____

* See relevant pages in this book: (48, 49). A list of CPCAs should be provided by your diocese. If not, dialogue and decide your own.
** A goal is a statement of something, within its capacity, which your parish intends to do or become in a three year timeframe.

ONE SUCH FORM IS TO BE COMPLETED FOR EACH CPCA.

Illustration 6.6

PROGRAM PROFILE

Parish:_____Place:_____Date:_____

Program #____* Critical Pastoral Concern Area (CPCA)

_____

1. Program _____

2. Program Content _____

_____

3. This is a current program we intend to continue as is ☐
   This is a program we want significantly to expand ☐
   This is a proposed new program in our parish ☐

   If this is an expanding or new program, describe briefly what is involved and planned in it: _____

4. Specify current and proposed (if the program is to be expanded or is a new program) budget, staff, etc.:

	CURRENT	IF EXPANDED	NEW
Staff (paid)	_____	_____	____
Volunteers	_____	_____	____
Budget	_____	_____	____
Estimated Number Served	_____	_____	____

5. This program is entirely administered ☐, staffed ☐, funded ☐ by our parish.

6. This program operates in partnership with another Catholic parish ☐, with one or more other churches ☐, with the civic community ☐. Specify with what group(s) you partner, how the program is staffed, and how the program is funded: __

---

* A program is a continuing activity in the parish, some purposeful and deliberate effort in which a number of parishioners is involved. Do not list here those usual sacramental and rectory services which are provided as a matter of course in all parishes.

ONE SUCH FORM IS TO BE COMPLETED FOR EACH PROGRAM.

CHAPTER SEVEN

REDISCOVERY THREE: FEELINGS

> Simple obedience is a thing of the past. . . . People today
> expect to know why things are done the way they are. They
> also want to be part of the decision-making process.[1]

Since World War II we have become progressively more
concerned about how we are and how we relate. In the same
timeframe, our capability for self and relational analysis has
mutltiplied massively. Analytic hardware and software
abound. This highly sophisticated introspection has let loose
an information explosion. Both in data and in the mechanics
for dealing with it we can now probe as never before our
singularities and our connections.

By a fortuitous or, perhaps, providential coincidence,
all of this occurs at a moment when the Church, too, re-
examines itself and proposes *aggiornamento* or update:

> Perhaps God through the (Vatican II) Council has providen-
> tially allowed the Church to modernize its mission at the
> very point in time when the technical means exist for mod-
> ernizing its method. . . . The resources of the Church . . .
> need to be mobilized, coordinated, stimulated and directed
> toward the most significant goals and the most effective per-
> formance.[2]

This was written, not surprisingly, in the very year when
the first two diocesan pastoral planning offices were

established—in the Archdiocese of Baltimore and in the Diocese of Pittsburgh! The chief resource of every organization and every institution is its people. If now we can canvass them with many new ways and wisdoms the rationale and the urgency for so doing remain no less fundamental than they ever were. It is to that urgency that this chapter responds.

The third dimension in REDISCOVERY is, thus, feelings —subjective data. How do the people with whom we share and plan feel about our common adventure? The only sure method for finding this out is to ask them. Emerson suggested once that there is a kind of optical illusion about every person we meet. So, too, unless they tell us directly, we can very easily be misled by what we think people think. We canvass them

- because we want to direct our corporate energies toward the subjective realities in our congregation;
- because we need to identify the aspirations, preferences, and frustrations which currently inhabit our pews;
- because the more people are involved in the process, from the beginning, the more likely it is they will do what is planned—and with greater enthusiasm.

Planagement literature in this matter is unanimous, e.g.,

While we share the same reality with others, we each tend to see that reality in our own terms.[3]

"We need to keep looking for the different mirrors that others use to perceive reality."[4] "Everybody always wants something . . . everybody is a special pleader."[5] Good managers and planners are always "listening, empathizing, and staying in touch."[6] As elsewhere, "people have multiple, often conflicting expectations of the church."[7] In short, again, we must accurately estimate and direct our energies not toward what we think our congregants think but toward what they tell us they think! Perhaps more so today than ever before, institutions plan well only when they recognize and accommodate "the primacy of the consumer."[8]

FEELINGS FIRST

Parishes need subjective data at various times and in varying dimensions. Here the focus is on feelings first, the gathering of subjective data as a comprehensive element in parochial REDISCOVERY. Necessarily this means a canvass process and appropriate instruments. There are these considerations:

1. Americans need to know up front *the whys and wherefores* when you poll them. As the process begins, as the instruments are distributed, your reasons for doing so must be widely communicated throughout the parish. The role and urgency of this phase in your total planning effort must be repeatedly emphasized.

2. Subjective canvasses are difficult and complex. Methodologies differ. Particularly if a parish is large and/or diverse, it is well advised to engage the guidance of a *local expert*, someone who is preferably professional both in preparing canvass instruments and in interpreting results. This person must, however, totally concur in the decided methodology. Otherwise, confusion will result.

3. Instruments must be brief, clear, and clean. The key word is KISS: Keep it simple, stupid! If they are too complex, ambiguous, and/or abstract, the canvass is flawed.

4. The development of a good canvass instrument designed to surface first feelings is subject to many advices. Each has its pluses and its minuses. My own tested approach proposes that the instrument be one—or at least not more than two—pages. It is broken down into two categories: The first category is open-ended, what I describe as *free fall*. The second category is closed-ended, what I de-

scribe as *guided missile*. In the free fall category, two questions are posed: what are the strengths of this parish and in what areas does this parish need to improve? (see sample form, page 77, questions 1 and 2). Here respondents surface their own perceptions. There are no limits, no constricting semantics. In the guided missile category, specific parish persons, programs, organizations, and activities are listed. Respondents rate each good, fair, or poor (see sample form, page 78, question 3). Cumulating results in this category, the parish knows item by item how it is perceived in its pews. Parishes and/or dioceses may elect to add a third canvass category. This category is contextual. Respondents are asked to identify their perceptions of the parish as part and parcel of civic and ecclesial communities larger than itself (see sample form, page 79, questions four and five). Such a category does provide important information. But it may dysfunctionally elongate the instrument, and it solicits opinions on subjects with which many parishioners have little familiarity.

5. Canvass instruments must provide space for *respondent identification*, e.g., by age, sex, Mass attendance, possibly also income, and educational levels. This enables distinction by group. As far as feasible, such data should be machine-readable.

6. The canvass process should be freed up from any respondent inhibition. Nothing and no one should obstruct *an uninhibited response*. Instruments should be returned unsigned. Direct interviewings, even *viva voce* dialogue, certainly have their place in subjective canvasses, but there is inhibiting restraint in each of them.

7. *A leadership control group* should be identified and recorded. Pastors, staff, council members, etc., should be surveyed via the same precise instrument with which the

parish as a whole is canvassed. This can be done at a time other than that when all parishioners are surveyed. Or, in the course of that saturation survey, each leader can be instructed to place a large letter *L* at the top of his/her form. Comparing control group returns with those from other parishioners, an important initial dynamic results.

8. Parochial canvasses, whether or not they include the optional third category on their instruments, have a larger than local significance and utility. They can be extremely helpful to the region and diocese to which the parish belongs. For instance, by cumulating results, a bishop or a regional pastor can develop a grass roots profile of perceived strengths and areas for improvement in all local churches. He then knows far more accurately the reality to which he proposes to respond. This, however, can happen only if survey instruments are identical from parish to parish; thus the urgency for *one set of semantics and one canvass format* in each diocese.

Building from this rationale and these considerations, how do parish leaders best proceed to probe the feelings of their congregation?

WHAT? The survey instrument should be brief and simple, preferably one but not more than two pages. It should focus on the parish itself, though it may include contextual, civic, and ecclesial queries. Survey questions should be both open-ended (free fall) and closed-ended (guided missile), thus soliciting response in two dimensions. There must be no inhibition. A control group of parish leaders should be distinctly canvassed.

WHY? The rationale has already been amply noted. The benefits are many; the costs in paper and time are minimal!

WHEN/
WHO?
There are several options; each has its pros and its cons. In my view, particularly as a parish surfaces its first feelings, there is one compelling fact: any survey has two purposes. The first is, obviously, to gather accurate data. The second is to tell people: I cared enough to ask your opinion in this important moment and matter. Scientific sampling, house-to-house canvassing, etc., suffice for the first purpose. They do not sufficiently accomplish the second purpose. Only some form of very comprehensive polling can do this. Thus, I propose that the parish survey its people at all Masses on *a saturation weekend.* This should occur in place of the homily and with introductory remarks from the pulpit and in several preceding bulletins. I am well aware that there are flaws in this approach, but I know of no other equally effective alternative. This should be done as follows:

1) On the canvass instrument in the guided missile category, there should not be a "don't know" or "no opinion" column. True, some respondents will be unwilling or unable to answer on a particular item. But to provide them an easy out via such a column is to invite them to use that column. Better to let this happen when it happens than to encourage its practice.

2) Sufficient response time, at least fifteen minutes, should be made available at each Mass. There should be pencils in all pews.

3) Respondents should be explicitly urged to write particular comments on the reverse of the canvass form. Thus, additional free fall space is provided.

4) All forms should be completed and returned before parishioners leave the church.

CUMULATION

Guided missile category. Here *good, fair,* and *poor* responses can easily be tallied. There are various ways to rate and rank the results. I am not a social scientist. There may well be better approaches. Still I recommend this methodology:

    a. subtract *poor* from *good* responses, ignoring *fair* responses
    b. the resulting figure is the PRI on the item (Positive Response Index)

I remain unsure as to how best to factor in nonresponses. At least they should be noted. Here is how one item PRI calculation would look:

ITEM	Good	Fair	Poor	Responding (%)	PRI
3.1 Parish P. Council	40	20	15	75	25
3.2 Youth Ministry	10	30	45	85	-35

Obviously, the higher its PRI, the more positive the perception of the item in the pews. Again, I believe this method works sufficiently for the purposes desired. So long as one method is used throughout, I recognize the possibility of more scientific approaches. If the percentage of nonresponse is high, this may suggest the need for further public relations in regard to that item. By comparing PRIs, in any case, the parish quickly discovers where it is most and where it is least successful.

    Free fall responses, i.e., answers to questions one and two, and if asked, four and five, plus written comments. Here cumulation is more difficult. But not so difficult as may at first glance seem likely! In fact, the majority of free fall responses can be gathered under common headings. For example, if respondents identify "many volunteers," "a readiness to help," "involved parishioners," etc., these can be put together in a single category. If respondents identify "nothing for the kids," "little social activity for teens," etc., these too can be linked in a single category. Such a process of association, however, requires careful guidance to assure that all tabulators apply the same criteria.

POSTSCRIPT

To repeat, subjective REDISCOVERY is based on three observed facts: First, that planning parishes need to know what their people think and that this must not be presumed ("An individual's reaction to any situation is always a function not of the absolute character of the intervention but of his perception of it. It is how he perceives things that counts, not objective reality."[9]); second, that surveys have a dual purpose, one of which is to tell people that you cared enough to ask them at this critical moment—a saturation survey with both free fall and guided missile questions is the best way to accommodate this sort of purpose; third, that the more they are involved in a process from the outset, the more likely it is that people will respond to decisions and plans which emerge from that process—and with enthusiasm!

Note again, as on the instrument below, that space should be provided a) for parish leaders to identify themselves so that you can compare their opinions with those of the parish as a whole and b) for visitors to identify themselves so that you may separate out their opinions from those of your parishioners.

Illustration 7.1 (Appendix A.1)

SAMPLE SURVEY INSTRUMENT

REDISCOVERY: How Do You Feel?

As your pastor, staff, and pastoral councillors, we propose to rediscover this parish as a community of faith, grace, and service. We need to know how *you* feel. Please respond to each item below. Thanks!

i. I am female ☐,   male ☐

ii. I am single ☐,   married ☐,   separated ☐, a widow or widower ☐

iii. I am in high school ☐,   21 and under ☐, 22–35 ☐,   36–50 ☐,   51–64 ☐,   65+ ☐

iv. I have been in this parish for _____ years

v. I attend Mass weekly ☐,   daily ☐, occasionally ☐

DO NOT SIGN YOUR NAME

If you are a PARISH LEADER place an L in this box.
If you are a VISITOR place a V in this box.   ➡ ☐

1. These are the three principal STRENGTHS of our parish: (Please list the most important first, the next second.)

2. These are the three principal areas in which our parish needs to IMPROVE: (Most important first, next second.)

3. Rate each of the following as you have experienced it in the past three years or in the time you have been one of us:

	GOOD	FAIR	POOR
Weekend services (music, rites, etc.)	☐	☐	☐
Priest (leadership, ability, etc.)	☐	☐	☐
Homilies	☐	☐	☐
Parish staff	☐	☐	☐
Parish pastoral council	☐	☐	☐
Parish finance/administration council	☐	☐	☐
Sense of congregational community	☐	☐	☐
Religious education: grammar school	☐	☐	☐
Religious education: high school	☐	☐	☐
Religious education: adult	☐	☐	☐
School (where applicable)	☐	☐	☐
Youth ministry	☐	☐	☐
Outreach to newcomers	☐	☐	☐
Community outreach (service)	☐	☐	☐
Community outreach (peace/justice)	☐	☐	☐
Congregational giving: money	☐	☐	☐
Congregational giving: talent	☐	☐	☐
Parish social activities	☐	☐	☐
Facilities/grounds/maintenance	☐	☐	☐

*Please add or amplify any of the above responses
on the reverse of this form or on attached sheets*

Illustration 7.2 (Appendix A.2)

Optional

4. Our parish is a member of a *cluster of parishes* (deanery or vicariate). This cluster, as we benefit from and contribute to it, could be improved in these ways:

Our parish benefits from and contributes to our *diocese*. This relationship could be improved in these ways:

5. Our parish is a benefiting and contributing member of a neighborhood and a city/town. We could partner better with *our civic neighbors* in these ways:

Here is the way one midwestern parish cumulated and reported its findings in a saturation weekend canvass.

Illustration 7.3 (Appendix B.1)

Dear Friends,

On Saturday/Sunday, March 4/5, 1989 we took a "Growing A Better Parish" survey in place of the homily at each Holy Mass. We have tabulated the results of the 25 attitudinal items and you might be interested in the results. We appreciate the cooperation of those who responded; it will help our Committee greatly in projecting goals and objectives for the next five years. The "respondent profile" and the general comments are still being analyzed and we hope to have a report on them in due time. *1121 parishioners* and *301 visitors* responded. Not everyone indicated a preference on each item.

Item	Parishioners			Visitors		
	Good	Fair	Poor	Good	Fair	Poor
Weekend Masses: Liturgical components	859	212	15	211	57	1
Weekend Masses: Sermons	743	343	35	179	95	10
Weekend Masses: Music	622	355	98	157	97	27
Parish Priests: Availability	838	167	20	108	32	11
Parish Priests: Leadership	824	162	23	142	27	6
Parish Staff	731	223	22	100	34	1
Parish Council Performance	575	282	26	57	25	2
Committees/Organizations Performance	644	286	18	61	22	1
Sense of Congregational Community (warmth, friendliness, etc.)	644	379	66	170	66	5
Parish Organizations Accessability	534	239	30	80	31	2

Item	Parishioners			Visitors		
	Good	Fair	Poor	Good	Fair	Poor
Religious Education/ St. _____ School	635	183	39	53	18	4
Parish School of Religion (PSR)	403	182	43	36	17	6
Adult Religious Education	645	142	35	63	16	5
St. _____ School (general academics)	651	166	35	56	12	6
Community Involvement	579	323	38	85	32	1
Outreach to Newcomers, Congregation	557	355	89	133	63	16
Outreach to me (sense of belonging)	587	354	113	114	62	21
Inter-Faith dialogue and action	376	363	47	62	43	12
Congregational giving— Money	792	214	14	105	30	5
Congregational giving— talents, time	660	272	30	74	30	2
Church Spiritual Activities	783	190	20	98	34	4
Church Social Activities	685	282	34	84	38	6
Facilities	860	162	13	215	29	4
Grounds	724	285	71	206	43	9
Maintenance	693	312	64	187	37	4

Once again, our sincere thanks to all who took the time to respond to this survey. We do appreciate it.

Illustration 7.3A (Appendix B.2)

Number of Comments on the Strengths of the Parish				
Item	Total	1st	2nd	3rd
1. Priests	290	154	82	54
2. School	282	76	118	88
3. Variety of activities, organizations, etc.	229	60	95	74
4. Facilities/location/size	152	51	46	55
5. People	127	42	47	38
6. Active participation/ volunteers	107	45	45	17
7. Liturgy	92	54	22	16
8. Sense of community, belonging	89	53	20	16
9. Leadership	85	55	19	11
10. Adult Education	80	25	30	25
11. Financial support/resources	77	25	34	18
12. Pastor	75	48	18	9
13. Hospitality	75	24	26	25
14. Spirituality/opportunity for growth	62	30	17	15
15. Mass schedule	56	18	22	16
16. Homilies	48	16	19	13
17. Music	37	9	14	14
18. Athletic program	21	3	7	11
19. Outreach to needy, disadvantaged	21	4	10	7
20. Lay leadership	18	3	12	3
21. Progressive, open-minded parish	18	6	12	-
22. Self-evaluating, improving	18	6	12	-
23. Father _____	17	9	6	2
24. Staff	14	8	3	3
25. Art	14	1	7	6
26. Well-organized parish	12	8	-	4
27. Community involvement, outreach	10	-	-	10
28. Young people/CYC/SYAG	10	-	5	5
29. Miscellaneous (less than 10 each)	14	62	11	37

Number of Comments on Areas Needing Attention

Item	Total	1st	2nd	3rd	Comments
1. Outreach/ Hospitality	420	209	98	51	62
2. Liturgy	303	96	78	45	84
3. Music	279	109	94	57	19
4. School	228	99	59	41	29
5. Maintenance/ Facilities	203	94	60	40	9
6. Programs wanted	175	60	36	31	48
7. Homilies	159	74	38	28	19
8. Other	178	13	20	18	127

All of this will require time for further analysis in order to ascertain the directions in which we should go. We thank all who made comments; they will be carefully weighed in planning for the future.

[1] Larry W. Kennedy, *Quality Management in the Nonprofit World* (San Francisco: Jossey-Bass, 1991) 53, 54.

[2] Patrick O'Meara, *America* (June 10, 1967) 837.

[3] Robert H. Schaffer, *Business Horizons*, April 1971, cited in an Indiana University Graduate School of Business reprint, 3.

[4] Robert H. Waterman, *The Renewal Factor*, (New York: Bantam Books, 1987) 173.

[5] Tom Peters and Nancy Austin, *A Passion for Excellence* (New York: Random House, 1985) 7.

[6] Peter F. Drucker, *The Effective Executive* (New York: Harper and Row, 1966) 150.

[7] "Model of the Church in Ministry and Mission," Center for Parish Development, Naperville, Illinois, 1979, 25.

[8] John Naisbett and Patricia Aburdene, *Megatrends 2000* (New York: Morrow and Co., 1990) 307.

[9] Rensis Likert, cited in Ross A. Weber, *Management* (Homewood, Ill.: Irwin Inc., 1975) 179.

CHAPTER EIGHT

REDISCOVERY FOUR: CONTEXT

The fourth component of parochial REDISCOVERY is context. Parishes, like people, are not isolates. A parish is part and parcel of wholes larger than itself. In this stage of its planning progress, the parish—as it were—rediscovers the seas in which it swims. It probes and enunciates its ecology. Ecology is the science of relationships. Ecology responds to a fundamental fact. Each living organism impacts on and is in turn impacted by the living organisms around it. I call them adjacencies. In the process of its ecological REDIS-COVERY, a parish identifies those adjacencies which substantially impact on its future—and vice versa. One set of adjacencies is civic, the other ecclesial.

CIVIC CONTEXT

Increasingly, we Americans pool our public resources and responses. Schools, banks, news media, etc., more and more operate on a regional basis. Metropolitan districts provide us with transportation, sewage disposal, water, power, and such. We shop in regional malls. At the same time many of our societal opportunities and problems require larger-than-local action. As the parish explores adjacency, it reckons in two dimensions. It benefits from its public relationships—it should contribute to them. Likewise, as it inspires and helps equip its lay congregants as "apostles in the marketplace," it needs itself to be closely aware of the actualities and prospects of that marketplace.

What kind of data? Parish leaders will pose and cumulate answers to questions like this:

1. What is the current demography of our neighborhood, city/town, county, state? What trends?

2. What are the current economic and social realities in our area? What trends?

3. What "justice and peace" situations exist in our area which demand the application of a "larger gospel"? Who now does what, how, and when? What trends?

4. What public projects and plans are now underway in our area, e.g., land use, highways, etc.? What trends?

5. What are we and proximate churches now doing to impact on the civics of our area? What prospects?

How does the parish surface such data? It does so by reviewing appropriate papers and dialoguing with appropriate persons. These categories:

1. Political, economic, and "development" papers and persons

2. Health and welfare papers and persons

3. Relevant state papers and persons

4. Regional utilities, school district papers and persons

What next? Parish leaders first record critical current data. This in staccato fashion, clear and clean! They summarize and communicate this data in the final REDISCOVERY report. They then reflect on prospects. What seems likely to happen in our civic adjacencies in the foreseeable future? They develop a change profile. All seemingly likely changes are recorded. Each is given a target date. Each is rated in terms of its probability. A number five, for example, indicates that in the view of parochial leaders, this change is very likely to occur, a number one that, while it is possible, it seems unlikely; the numbers two, three, and four indicate a degree of probability ranging between the two extremes. Here is what a parish change profile might look like:

Illustration 8.1

Change	Target Date	Probability
A. 450 new service jobs in our area	1998	4
B. Expansion of a 2 lane ring road around our city/town to 4 lanes	2000	2
C. An ecumenical food kitchen downtown	1995	5
D. Local auto plant closes, 500 jobs lost	1997	3

This sort of change profile is also recorded, appropriately digested, and placed in the final REDISCOVERY report.

Bridges. This kind of contextual, ecological identification of its adjacencies provides a parish with important data. But it has a major additional advantage. In the process, parish leaders have built bridges to key public persons and offices. As they walk these bridges in the future, the way is familiar. Likewise when the walk begins from the other side!

ECCLESIAL CONTEXT

> It is becoming increasingly clear that in many areas—youth, family life, special celebrations—our parishes are called upon to find new ways of cooperation and collaboration to make their work more effective.[1]

The second set of adjacencies is ecclesial. Here the parish probes its relations with a) proximate Catholic parishes, b) proximate churches of other denominations, and c) the hierarchy of operations and consultation as it exists in the diocese. The need for this contextual analysis is substantial and growing. The impetus toward pooling has three principal components. The first is sacerdotal. We are increasingly short of priests. True, pastors no longer sing solo. They work with staff and "ministers," councils and commissions. They enable ministries. Still, they remain indispensable. Their numbers shrink. They age. They are often over-extended. They confront massive expectations. Even with professional assistance and advice they cannot be everywhere and do everything. The second is lay. To practice lay ministry in a contemporary parish requires much training. To cover each base on which lay ministry seems indicated often requires fiscal resources well beyond the capacity of single parishes. The third is a consequence of the first two. To ponder and accommodate the revolution of instant expectations in their pews, individual parishes must more and more reflect on the possible pluses in some sort of pooling with proximate parishes. They must at least consider how certain things they now do alone might better be done on some kind of a regional basis.

It will be helpful to delineate many of these ecclesial considerations as they are phased and phrased in several contemporary American (arch)dioceses!

A. *Dubuque.* On April 12, 1992 at the end of a massive effort in "Archdiocesan Pastoral Planning," Archbishop Daniel W. Kucera, O.S.B., listed several reasons which apply to parish planning generally; but, particularly, to the urgency for regional thinking:

> Why parish changes? We have seen the signs of the times in the headlines in the past few years. A shortage of vocations to the priesthood; pastors who are overburdened with the care of several parishes with much travel between; a shift in the Catholic population and in some areas a decline; the mobility of the American public; the effects of economic

recession and the need to practice careful stewardship with our Archdiocesan resources.

In the same issue of his archdiocesan paper, a specific regional objective is stated:

Each parish is to list areas of current collaboration and indicate choices for future collaboration should it be necessary for linking or clustering with other parishes.

B. *Milwaukee.* As he initiated a substantial parish planning effort, Archbishop Weakland wrote:

Even if there were an ample number of priests, lay people would both have a right and a duty to minister in the Church. It is exciting to think about what a wonderful world we could have if we had a continual increase of both priestly vocations and the realization of lay vocations to ministry in the Church and the world.[2]

That effort requires:

(That) each parish, in conversation with neighboring parishes or a district (deanery) suggest ways to further collaborate, cluster or consolidate, so that the available priests and well-trained lay people can be of effective service.[3]

The effort was to be implemented in three stages:

1. Parish Study . . . analysis of parish mission (and) suggested models for the future which involve collaboration with other parishes;
2. Neighorbood Parish Study . . . agreement on workable collaborative models among neighboring parishes considering the needs and resources of the people;
3. District (deanery) Study . . . neighboring parishes . . . plan as a district, including several possible models.[4]

C. *La Crosse.* In 1989–90 we took a somewhat different but still regional approach. As consultant, I visited each of the fourteen deaneries. The given in our dialogue was a possible decline in clerical numbers of 25 percent by the year

2000. How, if this happened and in the light of the situations in the parishes, would the deanery deal with this decline? If it now had eight priests, how would it place six, etc.? I met with priests in the afternoon and with a large group of representative laity from deanery parishes in the evening. When I left, the Bishop had before him fourteen homegrown recommendations as to how he should place his parish priests if, indeed, the 25 percent decline occurred. True, a diocese is a patchwork quilt of which each deanery is only one patch. Local preferences can never be entirely accommodated. Still, priests and people had been convened to reflect on their local and regional realities and to think together as to preferred futures.

D. *Joliet.* In Joliet in 1990–91 we were confronted with the increasingly obvious need for realignment in the See City. The Diocese was growing massively in its northern reaches, e.g., Du Page County. It was static in its rural south. Joliet itself was immersed in what seemed to be increasingly dysfunctional ecclesial nostalgia. Most of its parishes had very deep roots in a proud ethnic past. While the population remained at best constant, there were nearly one hundred Masses, often at the same time, in twenty parishes each weekend. There was, obviously, an insistent demand for more priests to the north. To meet the challenge, we set up the Joliet Area Study (JAS). It was advised by a Steering Committee chaired by the Auxiliary Bishop. It involved several meetings with local clergy and four large assemblies of laity, priests, and religious. We asked them, having first canvassed the current and prospective facts in each Joliet parish, to come up with recommendations as to how the city might place fewer priests in the future. Joliet, we suggested, was a canal city with active locks. The task, then, was to raise the level of our collective thinking and planning from single parish to overall ministry. The end result was that we endorsed the idea of what we called "pastoral groups." We invoked and shared this kind of wisdom:

> While the parish remains the primary institution of our communal Church life, it cannot of itself meet all the pastoral needs of the community. . . . Any structural reform must concern itself with the renewal of present structures and the creation of new structures.[5]

On February 19, 1991 participants in a large JAS assembly voted as top priority that "we must begin to do more things together." Responding to them, our final recommendations were that

> Each parish in the Joliet area should become part of a pastoral group, These groups would be charged *first* to look together at pastoral needs, opportunities, and resources in their respective group areas. *Second,* to assess the capacity of parishes within their group to staff and otherwise resource the identified needs. *Third,* to identify needs which should be met rather on an area-wide basis by several groups. *Fourth,* to activate such responses and resources as are feasible within the group and to evaluate them at the end of the year.[6]

But we could not rely on our paper plan to happen unaided. Islandism might again triumph over the challenges of collective change. We called for an on-going JAS Steering Committee with an annual pastoral assembly with elected delegates from all parishes. We likened this to oxygen:

> The kind of widely participative effort which this (JAS) Study has been is a fire which requires such continuous oxygen and notice.[7]

We left the precise delineation and location of pastoral resources and accountabilities within each group to the discretion of its pastors and people with one major exception: Youth ministry, in all its dimensions, we saw as something which required action "on an area-wide basis."[8]

In its approach to implementing the study, Joliet might consider using a matrix technique. Each pastoral group would ponder and complete a form like this (items specified below are indicative not exhaustive):

Illustration 8.2

Pastoral Group: _____ Plan/Action Matrix

> Reflect on these pastoral concerns.
> Assign each a letter as indicated below.

(a) This should remain local, i.e., in each group parish.
(b) This should be done by two or three group parishes in concert—the other group parishes, as feasible and appropriate, assisting in funding and staffing it.
(c) This should be done on a group-wide basis, all parishes assisting in funding and staffing it.
(d) This should be done on an area-wide basis, i.e., in concert with another or, perhaps, all groups in the area.

1. **Masses**
   Daily _____
   Weekend _____

2. **Sacramental Preparation**
   First Communion _____
   Marriage _____
   RCIA _____
   Baptisms—infant _____
   Baptisms—other _____

3. **Penance**
   Individual _____
   Communal _____

4. **Justice and Peace**
   Service _____
   Prophetic _____

5. **Youth Ministry**
   Catholic school(s) _____
   Catechesis grade school _____
   Catechesis high school _____
   Social-cultural/athletic etc. _____

On the basis of the preferences which surface, group, priests, and people then flesh out procedures to accommodate or change them. Where the *preference* is (b), (c) and/or (d), clear and clean lines of responsibility, joint funding, and staffing should be specified and fully agreed upon before any such combination approach is implemented.

E. *Providence.* Though they were written nearly two decades ago, the words of Bishop Gelineau remain as true today:

> We need to overcome the isolation that has become in our day a hindrance to the mission of the Church. . . . The deanery is the natural location for many things to happen. I hope it can become a real connection between the responsibilities I have to the universal Church and the day-to-day work of the Church, which is for the most part carried on in the parishes. For example, I see diocesan departments more and more providing services on a deanery basis. The deanery is also the logical place to establish communication and collaboration between parishes.[9]

While, therefore, there has been a relatively widespread recognition of the need for some form of regionalization between the Church as diocese and the Church as parish, the practice has been less than encouraging in most places. Despite en route "guidelines" and high hopes, problems remain. First of all, it would appear that a great number of appeals for "collaboration" fall short. A few instances:

1. Many do not sufficiently stress the civic dimension, the parish as partner in commonwealth. Many propose intra-denominational partnerships but neglect larger ecumenical opportunities.

2. Despite the residual weakness of intradiocesan regions, many synods ignore the need for regional rethinking and reinforcement. They content themselves at best with innocuous *en passant* references. If this is to be expected in synods which deal only tangentially with structural

problems anyhow, it is nevertheless unfortunate in a Church where pooling is more and more obviously urgent.

3. Diocesan demographies and geographies change. Yet regional lines often remain immutable, irresponsive to new realities and connections. In other places, deaneries are supplemented by smaller groupings known as clusters, but insufficient notice is given to resulting ambiguities. And problems remain. How large or small should a Church region be? Should suburb and city be linked in a pie-shaped format? Should the regional Church, like its diocesan and parochial counterparts, be now conceived and practiced as inclusive of all elements in its People of God, or continue, as too often happens, entirely sacerdotal?

4. Both the upward and downward linkages of regional pastoral councils are frequently ineffectual. There is little communication in either direction and even less action. Many become, in fact, moribund. This seriously weakens diocesan councils and makes pooling polity much more difficult.

Diocese. In an hierarchic Church, the diocesan connection is fundamental. As a parish plans it must reflect on this two way connection: How does it benefit? What should it contribute? Consider these questions:

1. What emphases and/or major programs is our diocese now proposing? What is our response? How, if at all, should we change? Who, what, when?

2. Are the messages from our pulpit and pews getting through to chancery? Are we now adequately served by central offices? Do we now adequately respond to their requests? If not, on any count, what change?

3. How do we now relate to diocesan advisory bodies, and vice versa? Do we adequately communicate? Do we

promptly respond to their requests for input? There will be instances in which a parish can or should do nothing more than it now does. But, at least, it must ponder each of the above items and, where appropriate, deal with them.

Ecumenics. As it ponders its ecclesial ecology, the parish needs likewise to reflect on possible partnerships with its church neighbors. Much of this may be rather civic than spiritual. Still, the parish needs to know what these neighbors are doing and what all of them might better do together. Here again the parish builds bridges. It goes to the parishes around it and asks them about their emphases, programs, possible avenues for collaboration. One question could be: What do you think about us as a Christian community? How might we with you become a better institutional citizen in this place? This is not a matter of theology, polity, and liturgy but a practice of what former Mayor Ed Koch did when he went around New York City asking "How am I doing?" Admittedly, such a query is delicate, but it just might result in useful information from presumably benevolent outsiders. And ecclesial as well as civic bridges are important!

CONTEXT AUDIT

The performance of a system depends more on how its parts interact than on how they act independently of each other.[10]

Each parish is part and parcel of two systems or wholes, one civic, the other ecclesial. In its contextual probing, each parish surfaces data realities and prospects. It does a context audit. It records this audit. The audit, to summarize, communicates throughout the parish important information concerning the civic and ecclesial systems in which it locates, such as:

- Present and projected demographics
- Present and projected plans, economics, and "development" patterns

- The likelihood of changes in the parish area
- Health and welfare, justice and peace patterns and possibilities
- Major thrusts in mission and ministry in the diocese
- Communication, support, and action relationships between the parish and the diocese
- Major thrusts in mission and ministry of neighboring Catholic parishes, and opportunities for increased partnership
- Major thrusts in mission and ministry of neighboring churches of other denominations, and opportunities for increased partnership

All of this data is carefully collated, reviewed, digested, and made into a context audit which is included in the final REDISCOVERY report. Finally, in both civic and ecclesial dimensions,

> parishes exist within neighborhoods, towns and regions. Parishes have responsibility, together with other institutions and groups residing in an area, for the overall well-being of the community.[11]
>
> Parish communities (should) come to a realistic assessment . . . of their need to regroup in relation to other parish communities. . . . The process of clustering will require not only adjustment but creative adaptation on the part of pastors.[12]

[1] "Parish Pastoral Planning," Archdiocese of Portland, Oregon, 18.

[2] "Walking Together," Archdiocese of Milwaukee, August 1989, 34.

[3] Archbishop Rembert Weakland in "Walking Together," iii.

[4] Ibid., 1.

[5] "Adult Education—Adult Church," National Advisory Committee on Adult Education, Canadian Catholic Conference, Ottawa, 1986, 50, 60.

[6] Joliet Area Study, "The End of the Beginning," May 15, 1991, 1.

[7] Ibid., 4.

[8] Ibid., 3.

[9] "United in Hope," Diocese of Providence, cover letter, 1974.

[10] Chris Argyris, *Management and Organization Development* (New York: McGraw Hill, 1971) 18.

[11] "Parish Pastoral Planning," 18.

[12] "A Shepherd's Care," National Conference of Catholic Bishops, 1986, 49.

CHAPTER NINE

DOWN THE RECKON ROAD: ENGAGEMENT

THE LOCAL MEDICI

The Medici ran Florence for centuries. They administered. They presided at festivals. They filled the key slots in governance. No doubt, they chaired all significant boards. I call similar persons in a parish its local Medici. Why? Because the term says precisely what I mean. And it is memorable!

The local Medici are those who "are always there." The pastor can count on them to do things, to come to meetings, to attend diocesan sessions as parish representatives. They staff the parish. Many of them play musical chairs. Knocked off one committee by the rules, they simply join another committee—and so it goes. Now and then, of course, non-Medici faces surface. Now and then, non-Medici people are elected. But by and large, it is a local Medici group which constitutes the leadership core in most every parish. This has obvious disadvantages. It also has advantages. The local Medici, for whatever reasons, are personally invested in the parish. Their long-term involvement familiarizes them with the style of the pastor, with budget realities, with resource capacities, with staff idiosyncrasies, with context, etc. They get things done. They are available when a harried pastor needs someone to send to a diocesan event. Negatively, they tend to close in on themselves. They can become possessive, exclusive, disdainful of "newcomers." The fact remains, in most North American parishes, participation is first and foremost an activity of the local Medici!

ROLE

Engagement is that stage in a parish progress down the RECKON ROAD which co-opts the local Medici. They are deliberately brought into the picture, plus, of course, those non-Medici who may in one way or another now occupy some leadership positions in the parish. This is done for a very basic reason. If, in any planning process, those in local authority are bypassed, their experience and prerogatives ignored, they will subsequently either oppose what has been planned or find ways to tilt it otherwise than was intended. It is essential that the local Medici be stroked, affirmed, that their talents and immediate graces be brought early into the planning effort. There are these further advantages:

1. By involving the local Medici soon, they become comfortable with the planning process and feel good about it

2. By involving them soon, they become themselves facilitators who can move on to shepherd the parish as a whole through the same process they have so recently experienced

3. They sense an ownership of the process which will later inspire them to even greater loyalty to corporate goals and horizons

4. To move directly from raw data to a full-blown plan is counterproductive (This is particularly true when and as the parish as a whole is to be activated in the dialogue process. Far better to refine that data first than to dump it unrefined on a total parochial table! And what better group to do precisely this than the local Medici?)

It has been suggested that the health of any organization can be measured by the direction in which the psychic energies of its middle managers flow. In ENGAGEMENT such energies are deliberately solicited, informed, and put to work in early dialogue of a preferred parochial tomorrow.

PROCESS

All parish leaders, every one of the local Medici, are identified and convened. Who are they? Pastor and staff, obviously, plus members of pastoral and administrative councils, school board, etc., plus anyone else who believes he/she is a leader! These leaders gather in prayer. They review REDISCOVERY data in all its four dimensions. They note particularly how, in the canvass of feelings, their own responses may or may not have differed from total pew responses. They conclude appropriately: What does all this data say to us? How can we best respond to it? What challenges, what opportunities, what partnerships? They propose an initial parish mission statement.

After this sort of analysis and dialogue, the local Medici develop certain germinal parochial goals (see Appendix A). These are three year targets fleshed out with ballpark resource estimates. They then develop a set of objectives—one year targets—in association with these goals. Here, too, the suggestions are germinal and ballpark rather than fully detailed (see Appendix B). When they have done so, the local Medici put all their recommendations into a report which is then reproduced and widely circulated.

CAUTION

The local Medici proposes; the parish as a whole, under the guidance of its pastor, decides. True, leadership wisdoms as they surface in ENGAGEMENT are of great importance and should be appreciatively received. But they must not become intransigent. The decisive role in parish planning rests with the People of God. It is of the utmost urgency that this fact be kept in mind—and particularly by the local Medici themselves—throughout this leadership involvement progress down the RECKON ROAD.

Goals/Objectives

A goal is something this parish has decided it will do or become within a three year timeframe. Each goal must relate to a Critical Pastoral Concern Area (see pages 112, 113). A list of such CPCAs should be provided by the diocese. Otherwise, it is developed by the parish itself before it proceeds further in its planning. Each goal must:

1. Lie within the *capacity* of the parish to implement with no more than a reasonable stretching of its current and prospective resources

2. Be as *measurable* as possible (For instance, a good goal might be to double the number of regular participants in our high school religious education program. To improve our high school religious education program would not be a good goal.)

3. Be *consonant* with other goals, i.e., not competitive or contrary to the purpose of all parish goals

4. Begin with an *action* verb (see #2 above)

How many goals? There is no fixed ideal. The spinning off of too many goals is, however, counterproductive, particularly if there is no priority differentiation among them. Better one or, perhaps, two goals in each CPCA than a whole flock of goals, none of which is prioritized. Remember, any workable system of priorities requires a) posteriorities, and b) executive courage and fidelity in implementing it. One year before three year goals expire, progress to date should be carefully evaluated and new goals proposed to succeed them.

An objective is a one year program intended to advance a goal. Each objective must be *measurable, assigned,* and *broken down into action steps.* Each objective must lie within the *capacity* of the parish to accomplish it with only a reasonable stretching of its resources. If some resource commitment is well beyond what is now or will be available, the statement of that objective must include an explicit indication as to how this new resource will be engaged. Here, a few good objectives are better than many. Objectives too should be prioritized (see pages 137–139). As each objective reaches toward conclusion, e.g., at the half year mark, progress should be carefully evaluated and new objectives proposed. See the following form for a completed sample objective statement form:

Illustration 9.1

ARCHDIOCESE OF PORTLAND IN OREGON	*Pastoral Center*

THE ROLE OF THE GOAL
(see also "How to Grow a Better Parish," Rev. Robert G. Howes, Alba House, Canfield, Ohio 44406-0595, (216) 533-5503. Complete packet—$13.95; manual alone—$5.00)

Definition: A goal is a statement, agreed to enthusiastically by pastor and people, of something this parish intends to do or to become not more than a given time (e.g., three years) after it has been proclaimed.

Before: Prior to writing a goal, a parish will carefully review its previously written mission statement and ponder its thrust.

In developing goals, a parish will first discuss and analyze its previous canvass, REDISCOVERY, of itself in these dimensions—

    a. the FACTS;
    b. how its people FEEL about it;

c. its CONTEXT, i.e., as a benefiting and contributing member of two larger communities, one civic, the other ecclesial.

As it reaches the final goal moment, a parish will have already—

a. reviewed all alternative approaches;
b. selected among these alternatives;
c. and prayed over its decisions.

Criteria: A good goal begins with an *action* verb, to do something. For instance, to double enrollment in our high school CCD/RE classes would be a good goal; to improve high school CCD/RE would not be a good goal. Likewise, as this example indicates, goals must be as *measurable* as possible. A goal must be within the *capacity* of the parish, with only a reasonable stretching of its resources, to accomplish. Goals should be *few* and effective rather than many and superficial. Goals should be developed in those areas of parish mission/ministry in which there is perceived to be the greatest *need for improvement.*

After: Each three year goal must be broken down into one year programs or projects. These are *objectives.* Each objective in turn must be *staged,* i.e., further broken down into specific accomplishment steps. It must be explicit, *costed*—what will this require in resources? It must be explicitly *assigned* to people or groups who are able, even enthusiastic, to do it. Obviously, each objective must be *measurable.* The parish must be in a position to know when it has accomplished it.

Goals and objectives are the action elements in planning.

GOALS ARE DREAMS WITH DEADLINES AND LIFELINES.

2838 E. Burnside Street,
Portland, Oregon 97214-1895
503/234-5334

Illustration 9.2

Critical Pastoral Concern Area #: _____

Objective—Start Time: ____ Objective—Complete Time: ____

GOAL #: ____: _____

_____

> OBJECTIVE #:____: _____
>
> _____
>
> _____

1. RESPONSIBILITY OF: _____

2. ROLE OF PARISH COUNCIL (if council or one of its active committees is not responsible): _____

3. RESOURCES (where any commitment is extraordinary, asterisk the commitment, and indicate below how you will manage to engage it):

Item Required in Program/Project	Person Hours	Facilities	Funds
3.1 _____	____	____	____
3.2 _____	____	____	____
3.3 _____	____	____	____

*How we will manage extraordinary commitment(s): _____

_____

4. SEQUENCE (Intermediate steps required to accomplish this objective):

Step	Completed by
4.1 _____	_____
4.2 _____	_____
4.3 _____	_____

5. COMMENT (add here any additional detail which will help your parish community better understand and accomplish the program or project which constitutes the core of this objective):

May be reproduced for Program use.

Illustration 9.3

(SAMPLE)   **Objective Statement Form***

PARISH: St. Robert   DATE: June 15, 1993
PLACE: Crossroads, USA

Critical Pastoral Concern Area: #2, Faith Formation

Objective: Start time: September 1, 1993
           End time: June 15, 1994

GOAL 2.1 To double the enrollment of those who regularly at-
         tend our high school religious education program

Objective 2.1.1
To train three couples in the contemporary content and best
techniques of high school religious education so that they
may constitute a leadership core in our high school religious
education program.

---

1. RESPONSIBILITY: Our Council Religious Eduation Committee in conjunction with Rev. John Doe, our parochial vicar

2. ROLE OF OUR PARISH COUNCIL: To hear and dialogue
   reports every second month from September to June

3. RESOURCES (in the fund category, asterisk once if no unusual
   demand is made by this objective on current and prospective
   parish fiscal resources; asterisk twice and explain if an unusual
   demand is in fact involved, indicating how these extra funds
   will be forthcoming)

Item Required in Program/Project	*Person Hours*	*Facilities*	*Funds*
Committee meetings, dialogue and decisions on implementation method	60	Hall	—
Publicity, start search for couples	10	—	—
Texts and teachers for couples	10	—	$60.00
Training sessions for couples	24	Hall	$60.00

(*No unusual funding required. Money already in our religious education
budget.)

4. SEQUENCE (intermediate steps required to implement this objective)

Step	Completed by
Agree on method for recruitment and training	October 1, 1993
Publicize, contact, and commit couples	November 15, 1993
Train couples (with diocesan aid)	March 1, 1994
Decide on texts, schedule teaching (content, dates, location) in next year	May 1, 1994
Order texts (and visuals) and begin publicity	June 15, 1994

5. COMMENT: We anticipate that these three leadership couples will teach themselves at least in the first year and become teachers of competent others in the years ahead. We believe that thus working through core couples is a good way to start improving our high school religious education program. In three years, we will review our experience.

- -

*The above page has been largely extracted from the author's book *How to Grow a Better Parish* (Canfield, Ohio: Alba House, 1986) 43–44.

CHAPTER TEN

DOWN THE RECKON ROAD: COMMITMENT

Ownership is an essential element in motivation.[1]

The dream has been dreamed. The data has been gathered and communicated. Parish leaders have reviewed it. In a written report, they propose one or possibly a few draft mission statements, draft goals, and draft objectives. The next step is COMMITMENT: to submit all of this to the parochial WIDER WE. The expectation is that through this kind of grass roots ownership, parishioners, staff, and pastor alike will feel increasingly motivated to fulfill what is ultimately planned. Again, recall Vatican II's "common effort to attain fullness in unity" ("Dogmatic Constitution on the Church" 13).

Napoleon said once that his Grand Armee succeeded because every soldier carried a field marshal's baton in his knapsack. Even the private was personally invested in that army. So too in COMMITMENT, the task is to recruit as many as possible of the local People of God to invest in a good parish plan. Even if total numbers are seldom likely, at least we will have widened the ownership—the WE—far beyond what it would be had we simply allowed the local Medici to write and decree their plan. Here is where the two elements in the Quantity Imperative most insistently apply!

ACTION STEPS

1. If the data from the four phases of REDISCOVERY has already been summarized and widely communicated, fine. If not, we do this now.

2. Simultaneously, we summarize and widely communicate the drafts from ENGAGEMENT.

3. We invite written input. We also announce a series of plenary parish meetings to dialogue and recommend a final plan. This is done well in advance and promoted with every resource at our disposal.

4. I suggest four meetings, though more will likely be necessary in large and/or complex parishes. At the first meeting, participants dialogue the purpose of the entire planning effort, its process, its expectations. They then review the proposed mission statement draft(s) and reach consensus. At the second meeting they review draft goal statements and, at least, begin to bring them to consensus. At the third meeting, with appropriate homework in between, they review draft objective statements, flesh them out further and, at least, begin to bring them to consensus. At the fourth meeting, with appropriate homework in between, they review, reedit, and finalize the format and content of the plan they then recommend to parish leaders.

5. The pastor and the parish council edit, publish, and then commission and communicate the plan at a memorable parish liturgy.

FURTHER EN ROUTE CONSIDERATIONS

1. When local or proximate talent in meeting management is available, it should be tapped. The person who moderates must, however, be totally familiar with and committed to the planning method, language, and schedule

(MLS) which the parish has selected. Any confusion, any mixed signals will exacerbate an already intricate situation.

2. It should be explicitly noted that while leadership drafts from ENGAGEMENT are important, they are just suggestions. They do, of course, matter. They are informed advices. They may be advocated by the leaders, but the parish as a whole must remain entirely free to alter or, even, replace them. Such detachment on the part of the local Medici may not always be easy. It is always urgent.

3. Parish leaders with experience serve as facilitators of the process.

4. How much of the meeting dialogue should be plenary, how much in small groups? This depends on the local situation, e.g., the size and complexity of the parish, number of participants, etc.

5. To assure precise understanding and continuity, major actions at each meeting should be summarized and communicated prior to the next meeting. This for both informational and promotional reasons.

6. If an apparent impasse develops, spiritual discernment is invoked. The debate is halted. There is appropriate prayer for guidance. Each side retires and reflects on all the reasons why the other side may be right. They then reconvene, better able to reach consensus. I leave further tactics in conflict resolution to those more expert in such matters.

[1] Lawrence M. Miller, *American Spirit and Visions For a New Corporate Culture* (New York City: Morrow, 1984) 75.

CHAPTER ELEVEN

DOWN THE RECKON ROAD: KEEP ON

Ask the Lord to bless your plans and you will be successful in carrying them out (Proverbs 16:3).

On a church bulletin board once in delta Louisiana, I saw a sign which read, "Pray for a Good Harvest, but Keep On Hoeing!" I don't know who said it or when, but it speaks a great common sense. Thus, I title this final phase in my parish planning process KEEP ON.

The die is cast. The plan is done, approved, anointed, and communicated. What next?

A plan is a principal inspiration and reference point. As the saying goes, it proposes a future by design not by chance. But we have long since learned that no paper is absolute. No paper is forever. Time goes on. People and things change. Round pegs curve square holes. No community, no business, no parish can write a "master plan" anymore and presume that everything and everyone will implement its every detail. Your parish plan too must be repeatedly revisited and adjusted forward. Your goals and objectives, for instance, have timelines. They expire. They must be replaced. Planned performance is seldom just as you assumed it would be. This too must be revisited before you plan further. Continual hoeing, in one degree or another, is thus urgent for a continual harvest!

Keeping on thus means *assessing* how planned *account-abilities* have in fact been accomplished. Keeping on means measuring the *currency* and the *effectiveness* of your plan. Remember: *Effectiveness = performance + satisfaction.*

The accountable person or group must feel fulfilled as the accountability is met. The parish as a whole must see satisfying results in the subject area.

KEY INGREDIENTS

1. ACCOUNTABILITY. Accountability is holding some person or group responsible for doing something, agreed in advance, in a given manner in a given timeframe. Accountabilities, in the light of the plan, are specified in job descriptions or charters. These are prepared after a careful canvass of existing accountabilities, and when it has been determined that accountable persons or groups are capable, willing, and even enthusiastic about assuming such responsibility.

2. EVALUATION. This is the process through which the effectiveness (performance + satisfaction) of an accountable person or group is measured. Has what was planned been done fully or in part? Have those who did it felt self-fulfilled in the process? In practice, evaluation is seldom well done. Only performance is measured; people feel "threatened" etc. Thus parishes must approach the evaluation event with much care. It must be abundantly explained that this event is positive. What parish leaders propose to do with evaluation data must also be clarified. Again, given this delicacy, the involvement of persons within or near the parish who are experts in such matters is important. There are three types of evaluation. (I use group terms below. Individual evaluation is, however, subject to the same logic and process):

   2.1 *Internal.* How does the group feel about its performance? Is it satisfied? Did it fully accomplish its accountability? If it fell short, why? What things helped it, what things impeded it? In the light of its experience, what subsequent goals and/or objectives does it propose to the parish in this subject area?

2.2 *External.* How many were served in one way or another as this accountability was accomplished? How do these, its customers, feel about progress to date? What pluses, what minuses? What subsequent goals and/or objectives do its principal customers suggest in this subject area?

2.3 *Overall.* In terms of total parish mission and ministry—in terms of the parish plan—was this accountability properly accomplished? If not, why not, how not? What goals and objectives are indicated in subsequent approaches to this subject area? What changes, if any, in polity and/or process would make it more likely that this accountability would be handled better in the future?

3. SEQUENCE. Calendars run out on plans, goals, and objectives. Reasonably prior to the expiration date on any and all of these, the council convenes, evaluates, agrees on, and decides a sequence. If a new plan is in order, the parish walks again down THE RECKON ROAD. If new goals and/or objectives are in order, the first step is REDISCOVERY. What are the relevant *facts,* e.g., what actually happened with earlier goals and/or objectives? How do those most closely involved and its customers *feel* about this subject area? In what *context,* perhaps more or less altered from what it was at the start, must these goals and/or objectives situate? The second step is ENGAGEMENT. Relevant parochial leaders convene and draft new goals and/or objectives. The third step is COMMITMENT. In some overt manner, the entire parish is summoned to review leadership drafts and agree on new goals and/or objectives in the particular subject area(s).

4. PARETO'S LAW. This law proposes that in any group of circumstances impacting on a situation, only a few are of maximum consequence. For instance, if worker absence occurs, many factors may be involved, e.g., sickness, home difficulties, workplace stress. And yet a canvass of company experience may discover, hypothetically, that stress and negative workplace are paramount, accounting for 75 percent of the absences. Pareto's law proposes that the company is well advised to devote most of its remedial attention to stress and workplace negativism. So too, as it progresses in its planning, a parish will soon uncover certain factors pro and con which impact most substantially on its success or failure. To KEEP ON effectively, it must then focus on those factors, letting others slide. It identifies, in short, its most consequential opportunities and difficulties; then it relentlessly deals with each of them!

5. PRIORITIES. Priorities are those items on which a parish decides to concentrate its energies in greater measure and effort than on other possible items. Two things are essential for priorities to work. First, simultaneously the parish must decide its posteriorities. With limited resources, what things will it now postpone or abandon so that more urgent things can get done? Without posteriorities, writing a list of priorities is an exercise in academic gymnastics! Second, parish leaders must bring continual executive courage to priority implementation. If, on the other hand, various end runs succeed in getting decided priorities abandoned, and resources are otherwise allocated than by priority plan, the whole exercise has again been academic gymnastics, and people will not soon rally to a similar priority event! How does one develop a list of priorities and posteriorities? A few quick suggestions:

   5.1 Begin by identifying the variables against which you will want to measure various program alternatives:

- cost/benefit return (A)
- urgency in terms of overall mission and plan (B)
- capacity of the parish, through only reasonable stretching of its resources (C)
- ramification—the degree to which this alternative will positively impact on other parish priorities (D)
- sequence, i.e., the need to do this in terms of what can happen better if it is done soon (E)

5.2 Each alternative approach is clarified and recorded. All approaches are then fed into a matrix like this:

Program/Variable	A	B	C	D	E
a._____					
b._____					
c._____					
d._____					
e._____					

Each program alternative is measured in terms of how well it accommodates each variable—this with a number from 1 to 5. Maximum accommodation is a 5, minimum a 1, with 2, 3, or 4 indicating accommodation somewhere between the two extremes. The parish may elect to weigh some variable more heavily than the others. If so, this variable weiqht is multiplied by the alternative number. Say urgency is given a weight of two, and the original alternative program number in this variable category is 3, the number to be ultimately recorded is 6.

6. PASTOR/STAFF. As a parish KEEPS ON, it maintains operational continuity with its plan through its pastor and staff (see also Council Cues, pp. 136–149). Here are some of the things in which pastor and staff will converge their plan accountabilities:

6.1 They will refer often to the plan, citing it as it impacts on their activities

6.2 They will continually be concerned to measure the effectiveness (performance + satisfaction) with which planned targets are met

6.3 They will periodically in one way or another canvass parish pews for current perceptions and preferences

6.4 They will raise antennas to pick up innovative methods for accomplishing their plan, and effecting partnering with their ecclesial and civic neighbors

6.5 They will adhere to decided parochial priorities, adjusting as feasible their ministries visibly to accommodate these

6.6 They will periodically convene with their councils to seek spiritual guidance as they progress

6.7 They will be concerned, as the time approaches when new goals and/or objectives must be agreed upon, to sequence these so as to maintain continuity with and to advance previous goals and objectives

6.8 They will recognize and practice annual parish assemblies and task forces as important ways to sustain and assure plan ownership and accomplishment by an ever WIDER WE

Establishing continuity and demonstrating progress in planning is always important but seldom quick or easy. It requires courageous and frank evaluation and update. It requires market analysis and canvasses. It requires careful coherence between resource allocation and planned priorities.

CHAPTER TWELVE

TAKING CHARGE OF A CHALLENGE

If a parish has a good plan, subsequent opportunities and problems can be reckoned with in terms of that plan. But what if there is no plan? How does such a parish take charge of a challenge? The same logic applies. The challenge is first conceptualized. The steps are:

1. Dialogue, develop, and define the challenge in writing

2. Identify and define in writing those few factors which, out of many, seem most likely to significantly impact on the challenge:

   > Change is most effective when it deals with the factors that have the greatest causal influence on the problem in question.[1]

3. Submit all of the above to prayer and spiritual discernment

4. Convey this initial challenge analysis to the group(s) which will then propose to the parish how this challenge can most effectively be handled. These accountable persons then proceed down a RECKON ROAD similar to that associated with a more comprehensive parish planning effort

5. They rediscover the DREAM. How, ideally, might we deal with this challenge?

6. They rediscover the FACTS. How has the parish to date handled this challenge? What relevant in-house habits and trends are there? Has a parallel challenge been handled with apparent success elsewhere? How?

7. They rediscover the FEELINGS. How do key parish advisory persons feel about this challenge? Perhaps also, a dialogue with focus groups is needed, and/or a particular canvass of the parish as a whole

8. They rediscover the CONTEXT. Are there directives and policies from the larger Church, e.g., diocese, which bear on this challenge? Does anything occurring now or in the future in the civic community bear on this challenge? Does anything occurring now or in the future in proximate parishes bear on this challenge? What, if any, partnerships seem relevant?

9. ENGAGEMENT. Parish leaders gather, reexamine the data, and select among possible alternative approaches, indicating goals and objectives

10. COMMITMENT. Leadership recommendations are presented in some manner and to whatever degree seems appropriate to the parish as a whole. This wider "we" dialogues and moves to consensus

11. KEEP ON. The agreed response is activated. It is tested and tracked for one year. It is then evaluated and appropriately adjusted forward

As with all *planagement*, what reads well on paper often descends into problems as it confronts "the human condition." We city planners used to joke among ourselves—if only there were no people to reckon with, we could enable magnificent urban communities! So too, any challenge response must reckon with human factors. A few practical guidelines:

A. *Myopia.* A Bostonian's eye view of America bulks the Hub unrealistically large and the rest of the country, particularly west of the Hudson, myopically small. Advocates of any specific challenge response may likewise tend to oversize their cause. And yet any response will require some sort of resource reallocation. We must, therefore, carefully estimate in advance what a proposed challenge response will mean in the totality of parochial resources and energies.

B. *Accountability.* We must estimate in advance who must do what if our challenge response is to be effective. This is best done if the parish has developed what I call an accountability profile. Who, now in fact—not just "by the book"—does what, how, and when in this parish? This kind of accountability profile is obviously important in a large planning process. It is important here too. It makes possible particular estimates as to how the workload of involved person(s) will be affected by a proposed challenge response. Otherwise we may overload the energy system necessary for that response to be effective.

C. *Explicit.* Nonrecorded ideas can be both vague and quickly forgotten. The discipline of the explicit requires that at point after point in the challenge dialogue, and especially in its outcome, data and decisions be committed to writing.

D. *Consumers.* These pages have repeatedly stressed the absolute importance of a consumer orientation. If this is so in a larger planning effort, it is likewise true in the dialogue of a challenge. How are those to whom our response is directed likely to perceive and receive it? Staff and key advisors may smell success ahead. But just as the proof of a product lies in the eating, so that response must taste good to those we want to consume it.

Marshall McLuhan warned once that the price of eternal vigilance is apathy. As we canvass the many challenges to which a parish might respond, we need ruthlessly to identify and deal with those which are potential of the greatest benefit to us and which seem likely to engage the enthusiasm and the resources of pastor, staff, advisors, and people. In a good plan, we have already done this. Absent a plan, we must again and again ask ourselves, how urgent is this challenge? Or, if we now undertake to meet it, however significant it may be, will it so crowd parochial energies and resources that the net result will be apathy?

[1] Chris Argyris, *Management and Organization Development* (New York: McGraw Hill, 1971) 176. (cf. Pareto's Law)

CHAPTER THIRTEEN

THE PASTOR FACTOR

> The priest is not a manager.
> Yet 80% of his work is managerial.
> Maybe that's part of the problem.[1]

What is the role of a good pastor in a truly sharing and planning parish? If the priesthood is increasingly "relational," how does he best insert himself in parochial networks? If he is not primarily ordained to be a manager, how does he effectively manage the many co-apostles and groups with which he ministers?

The literature is enormous. I make no pretense to having canvassed even most of it. Nor do I necessarily endorse each of the comments which surface below. I am neither a sociologist nor an expert in sacerdotal dynamics. I have, however, read a lot. I have likewise observed a lot in my quarter century of ministry in many North American places. In 1969, Dr. Arthur X. Deegan, then staff planner in the Archdiocese of Detroit, wrote a book titled "The Priest as Manager." In 1990, obviously with tongue in cheek, Jesuit Father Thomas Reese, after visits to each American archdiocese, suggested that the definition of the ideal pastor today might well be Jesus with an MBA! In between, there has been literally an immense amount of speculation.

Again, I am neither a theologian nor a canonist. My focus here is, rather, on the practical realities, the quandaries and the *planagement* dimensions of a good pastor in a sharing, planning parish. In so doing, I propose to develop an existential canvass which can usefully be melded with those other, more fundamental, dimensions in his contemporary priesthood.

Two actual instances to begin with: A few years ago an American archbishop told his priests,

> We can no longer run this Archdiocese like a Mom and Pop store. We need business smarts . . . but I hope we don't become too business-oriented.[2]

Clearly, a similar problem exists on the parish level. A major problem for pastors today is how to approach parochial doing and sharing with appropriate business smarts and yet not become too business oriented. In the late 1970s I met with the pastor and some one hundred parishioners in a goal-setting session in Michigan. They surfaced a number of concerns and identified responsive targets. I sat afterward with the pastor in the rectory parlor. He was kind but he was also blunt. "Fine," he said, "but they didn't tell me anything I did not already know." I hesitated momentarily, then said, "That's it, Father; they told *you*. For the first time in this good parish, a large number of your people has caught your vision. This, far from impeding you, reinforces your leadership role in many ways." Effective and continuously enlarged sharing, therefore, affirms the alert pastor!

I cannot, nor do I propose here to raise up or comment on every single matter bearing on the contemporary parish pastorate. A few initial considerations must suffice:

1. *Indispensability.* (See the author's article in "Pastoral Life," August 1992.) Pope John Paul II, in one of his Holy Thursday messages, warned priests against the "temptation to feel we are not needed." No person is, of course, indispensable, but every person needs to be needed! Priests too are subject to this "human condition." Yet in recent years many of the tasks which told a pastor he was personally necessary have been elsewhere assigned. On the altar, once magnificently solo, he is now part of a crowd. In the rec-

tory, where once he presided as a kind of solitary monarch, he is now part of a crowd. I am well aware of the longstanding distinction between "pastoral things" and "temporalities." Priests, the argument runs, should be more and more freed up from the latter so that they can concentrate on the former. And, so far as it goes, the contention is valid. But there are other factors which must be considered. A skilled pastor "enabling ministries" and conducting a parochial orchestra is one thing. A pastor who feels he is increasingly a fifth wheel in his parish is another. One priest, for instance, was asked his views on "team ministry." He replied, "We sit around the table on Monday morning. They decide what they will do. I do what's left over." This kind of psychic problem is complicated by the fact that one of the two services priests uniquely render—penance—is now very infrequently practiced. And the other—Mass—declines in attendance, perhaps even also in centrality, in many places. At the same time, the priest's "identity crisis" grows. As he ages, few follow him. The profession to which he dedicated so much of his person now attracts inadequate numbers. There is also what I have elsewhere described as the death of utopia syndrome. Inspiring, sanctifying, and equipping a parish as it reaches toward a better tomorrow remains a mission in the accomplishment of which priests feel needed. But it is no longer possible to envision, either in Church or in state, a quantum leap forward from where we are to some grand tomorrow. This is no less true in a parish than it is elsewhere:

> Organizations are so complex that it is often difficult for top management to articulate an understandable vision for the future.[3]

Nevertheless, again in both Church and state, we Americans are well into a revolution of instant expectations. For instance:

> (Priests widely testify to the fact that the) expectations of their people have risen dramatically in the past ten or fif-

teen years. . . . The unrealistic and even contrary expectations of people and bishops have created standards that
pastors, try as they might, could not always live up to.[4]

Caught between the sheer impossibility of utopia and the
urgency for immediate response to multiplying expectations,
even the best pastor is reduced to incrementalism, to slow
steps patiently. Marshall McLuhan suggested once that the
price of eternal vigilance is apathy. The net result of a pastor's plight between the constrictions of a much circum-
scribed future and continually insistent expectations may,
indeed, be inertia. Disillusioned from his high ordination
hopes and troubled by uncertainty as to the sacerdotal
tomorrow, the priest may simply settle back, hold the fort,
and wait—with minimal enthusiasm—for retirement.

2. *The Funnel.* Bishop Ottenweller years ago proposed
that the typical pastor sits under the spout of a very busy
funnel. Chancery and other demanding mail pours onto his
desk in dysfunctional quantity. If anything, as central offices
proliferate and regional imperatives increase, this funnel is
now bigger and more crowded. In one large diocese priests
told me (a) "we're swamped and smothered," (b) "we have
far too many offices . . . we're overstaffed," (c) "pastors
are dumped on and not adequately prepared," (d) "I get too
much mail from everyone and everywhere," (e) "to be what
the bishop expects—idealism—and still run the parish well
is very difficult," (f) "there is simply too much duplication
and bloat." In another diocese priests by a better than three-
to-one margin said that "while some paperwork is necessary, chancery is excessive in its demands." I have encountered similar attitudes often elsewhere in my ministry. Parish
priests, sprawling over many areas of accountability, com-
plain both of the papers with response deadlines and the
meeting demands which pour through their local funnels.
To mix metaphors, it is probably true, as one perceptive
pastor told me, that "there are a lot of priests who just don't
want to bite the bullet." It is certainly true that in a People

of God polity there must be much convening and "communication." Still, to whatever extent it may be applicable in beleagured rectories, one fundamental fact remains: to demand super performance by super persons at any key point in an energy grid is to risk power failure!

3. *Vision and Direction.* "The leader is the evangelist for the dream."[5] It has wisely been suggested that nothing is more anxiety producing than to be asked to give full-time attention to too many disparate tasks. Unless the several accountabilities of a pastor are somehow melded into an overall vision and direction, they can indeed become cancers of anxiety in his life. In one large diocese recently, priests by a seven-to-one margin called for "a statement of pastoral vision enunciated by their bishop after widespread consultation with all elements in the local People of God." I gather this entire matter under the umbrella term *vision and direction.* Even though the principle itself is agreed, there is much ambivalence in the practice. Some contend that sufficient vision and direction emerge from the Gospels, from Vatican II, from an omnipresent Spirit. Others, and particularly priests, contend that their bishops fail to enunciate and sustain a specific local vision into which they can consistently plug. Still others acknowledge a basic difficulty; one dean told me, "I agree that vision and direction are lacking here, but I don't know how you deal with this today in pluralism." Thus, there is a combination of varying views, all stressing the importance but many recognizing the problems of specifying a viable vision in this place here and now. Consider: On the one hand, effective vision and direction require prioritization. If everything is a priority, nothing is a priority. This entails the identification of posteriorities. Such intervention disturbs existing patterns. The result is tension. Effective vision and direction require standards. Progress toward incarnating the dream must be measureable. This means evaluation, more papers, more meetings. On the other hand, some priests have complained to me of

"too little freedom. Our bishop is a micro-manager. He wants his hand in everything." Despite their frequent plea for more episcopal guidance, priests remain among the most autonomous professionals in America today. How to insert a realistic diocesan vision and direction into these autonomies is a difficult job. Nevertheless, the kind of overarching criteria provided in a good vision and direction statement provides pastors with a means for systematizing their several accountabilities and, even more importantly, for measuring their accomplishments. This in itself is an affirming benefit not possible when a pastor is left with no visible paradigm against which he can rate his ministry. Indeed, some form of vision and direction much more substantial and specific than merely a periodic succession of pious platitudes should be a major concern of every bishop today, however hard it may be to enunciate and courageously sustain it:

> Out of the uncertainty and chaos of change leaders rise up and articulate a new image of the future that pulls the organization together.[6]

4. *Collegiality.* Many studies suggest that the priesthood in our time is increasingly "relational." As this expresses itself in parochial sharing and planning, I describe it as a movement from solos through quartets and octets (as now) to choruses (a parochial WIDER WE). Formerly, Father sang and danced solo, encountering "his people" on weekends mostly, otherwise running things as he saw best. At present he sings and dances with a limited number of ministers and advisors. The ideal remains an ever-growing quantity of parishioners who work with Father at being and doing the local Church. If the ideal of such expanded collegiality is surely sound, its practice has proven difficult:

> While many pastors had a deep commitment to collegial ministry, they lacked the skills or astuteness that only experience and training can bring.[7]

Back in 1970 I heard one bishop tell his priests, "we're in a whole new ballgame, Fathers." He was referring to parish councils and other collegial structures. The People of God are, indeed, a new playing field. But priests then and now seem widely unsure of themselves on this field. Even in the bishop's own diocese there is no evidence that parish councils flourish nor are they supported by any staff person! Besides,

> Many pastors still feel that most consultative groups have not relieved them of their responsibilities as much as adding another duty to their schedule.[8]

Some priests do respond well to the challenge of the new pluralism in their rectories and advisory groups. Others at best tolerate participation and still others continue troubled by its technicalities. They see a loss of control, they find it hard to keep all the several players in balance. At the same time, they too are caught up in a sense of hopelessness. There seems so little they or anyone else can do about this complicated world:

> Pastors can seldom control the forces that are changing American parish life. They can, however, respond creatively.[9]

Some priests do respond to the demands of an effective collegiality well. Others merely mark time, drifting into early retirement. Besides, only here and there, competent to nibble at tomorrow, they fall victim to the usual human preference for the status quo. They close in on themselves, enduring all the meetings and advices with little enthusiasm. They become, in the crowd with which they must now minister, brittle and as brief as possible.

5. *Tensions.* In his Holy Thursday message to priests in 1984, Pope John Paul II called this "a time of great tensions." All of the above in one way or another suggests stress and strain for the pastor. Suffice it to cite more particular items in pastoral tension:

Pastors experience a growing tension between their dual roles as shepherds and spiritual leaders on the one hand and administrators of finance, buildings and employees on the other. Pastors experience a growing tension from being the man in the middle between "the Church above" and "the Church below," between old and new expectations, between conservatives and liberals and between individual staff members and/or lay volunteers who are involved in "turf fights." Pastors experience a growing tension between keeping one eye on the long-range future and the other on the immediate needs of the parish.[10]

This observer adds two key questions:

How does a pastor measure his success? How can I prove to myself that I am a good priest and a competent pastor?[11]

A seminary rector identifies another source of tension:

(There is a) lack of cultural and Church support of the priest. It is hard for seminarians to sustain . . . when they are not sure anyone really cares or values what they are doing.[12]

A Protestant observer remarks:

Since management theories and skills were not taught in most seminaries, generations of pastors . . . have attempted to engage in the practice of ministry without having the benefit of a theology of church management, a working theory of church management and the skills needed for church management.[13]

An active young pastor, widely published and heard, writes:

(The clergy) all tell me the same story, the same two basic complaints. They do not sense any direction, any vision in the church they serve; there are no visionary and imaginative leaders, just episcopal and clerical politicians doing business as usual. The enterprise called the Church doesn't seem to be going anywhere. . . . Then comes the second lament. "No one up there (chancery) cares whether I live or die, what I'm doing, how or why." There's no fraternity, no caring, no affirmation. . . . There is no over-all plan, direction, inspiration, vision.[14]

He adds:

> Most priests lack the simple skills in dealing with people and groups. The (old) seminary curriculum trained the priest to perform. . . . But he was not trained to minister or promote the ministries of others: his skills do not lie in working with groups, listening and letting things happen. He brings this outmoded posture to new ministerial situations and this is bound to cause friction.[15]

Summing up, the typical pastor may feel the need to be but also the impossibility of being some sort of superman as he ministers, not perhaps unlike how city planners feel:

> (We planners require) the wisdom of Solomon, the heart of a prophet, the patience of Job and the hide of a rhinoceros.[16]

In any case, most observers resonate with these sentiments in one way or another. Listen to the conclusion of a recent national bishops' publication:

> The contemporary pastorate has become "a specialized ministry." Because of the unique demands made on the pastor, because of the variety and the cluster of skills required to do this ministry effectively, the pastorate is not just a generic priestly function. . . . Should (their) role be confined to the administration of the sacraments and preaching most pastors will experience significant adjustment problems.[17]

I do not, of course, know how our seminaries have responded to this kind of advice. I do know of one seminary which hosted in its annex a full-day Saturday session for parish councillors from around the diocese. And yet no seminarian was present and, apparently, no emphasis on the relevance of this conciliar day was promoted by seminary faculty! Nor can I estimate how much has effectively been communicated through programs for "the continuing education of the clergy." Surely there have been talks here and there. I wonder, though, if all of the above is sufficient!

Whatever the circumstances and concerns may otherwise be in a priest's life, sharing and planning clearly constitute a major element in that life. I suggest this kind of response:

1. *All roles and all relationships must be explicitly and agreeably defined.* Good plan processes and papers do more than specify workable goals. They also propose an infrastructure through which such goals can be reached. This, indeed, is a necessity which seems to have eluded many recent American synods. As the parish shares and plans, everyone in it needs to know his/her place and what is expected from him/her. What about "surprises of the Spirit?" They will come. They cannot be anticipated. Still, even so, a good parochial script requires a commonwealth of lyric and book. I do not for one moment suggest that by simply pampering everyone all a pastor's problems will be solved. I do suggest that concentric and explicit clarity in such matters— for advisory groups as well as for individuals—can go far toward reducing the stress of operational and advisory ambiguity.

2. *Democracy of Means.* I have already detailed this important methodology as it impacts on parochial polity and planning (see pages 34–37). Suffice it here to be briefly repetitive since it also impacts on pastors. If they fail to resolve early and explicitly the advisory decisive dilemma, they risk continual frustration on all sides. Using his decisive prerogative rather to declare ends than to decree every associated detail, the pastor challenges appropriate staff and advisory groups to decide these details. He thus diffuses the dilemma. A much wider sense of ownership pervades his associates. Participation becomes much more extensively attractive. Grass roots energies—which might well be repelled if Father dictates everything all the way—are tapped. So long as staff and councillors act within the limits of parochial resource capacity and conform to Church directives, the pastor need not and should not intervene. At the evaluation

stage, though, his will be, as always, one of the most authoritative voices.

3. *Vision and Direction.* If some pastors lament the absence of vision and direction from their bishops, so too some parishioners lament the absence of much vision and direction from their pastors. I have already identified some of the difficulties in responding to this kind of complaint. If it is somewhat easier in a parish than in a diocese, it is still hard. I refer here again to a viable vision not to a succession of pious platitudes—what I call fluff stuff. While sea changes in parochial inertia are not possible, the pastor can help parishioners select and then join them in working on those items which seem most likely to impact on their common future. Chunking, again, nibbling at tomorrow. Still, by moving ahead however slowly, the good pastor senses progress, is affirmed, and his people too experience growth. The net result is mutually reinforcing.

4. *Self-Confidence.* No paper can endow a pastor with a sense of accomplishment. Only action pursuant to an agreed plan, in which more and more of his parishioners with more and more enthusiasm participate, can do this. An old Chinese adage has it, of a good emperor people say afterward, he did this and that. Of a superior emperor people say afterward, we did it all ourselves! So too, the more he can carry his people forward with him toward horizons, whatever their contemporary limits, the better a pastor is. His success will be theirs and their success will be his. I know of no better way to assure that Father in his rectory is continually affirmed!

5. *Identity/Skills.* "Pastors today require skills and competences that can be identified and taught."[18] Neither this book nor any other words or workshops can fully provide such "skills and competences." Through more familiarity with *planagement* as it is now theorized and practiced, through educational programs in his diocese, through such

texts and teachers as are cited here, however, the pastor can begin to develop his own expertise in these now essential dimensions in his ministry. But he must want and be helped to do so. Where there is no will, there will be no walk! As priests feel their way forward in the now multiple sharing and planning aspects of their priesthood, equipping them more effectively to respond is both an affirmation and a necessity.

6. *Delegation.* The principle is simple and compelling: If a person cannot be everything, everywhere, and everywhen, he or she must delegate. Delegation involves both *subsidiarity* (i.e., recognition, applause, and partnerships with those to whom particular apostolates and missions have been specifically assigned) and *wholeness* (i.e., a judicious overview of such persons and tasks in the light of the total parochial situation and preferred prospects). Effective delegation thus requires a dynamic of the pastor which was not present to any substantial degree when he stood solo. True, the buck still stops at the pastor's desk. If his successes go too often institutionally unnoticed, he will be faulted if some aberration occurs. A few relevant observations: If at one time it could be contended that "the besetting sin of parish administration is amateurism,"[19] today pastors operate in tandem with professionals or, at least, paraprofessionals. They team with persons more or less expert in religious education, liturgy, finance, etc. Sometimes their respective "theologies" converge. Sometimes they do not. There may well then arise personal and, even, corporate tensions:

> When people with strong professional orientation take over managerial roles conflict between the orqanization's goals and professional loyalties often occurs.[20]

The question of judicious control becomes critical. Here too many precise "skills and competences" are urgent. Here too a good parish pastoral plan in which relationships and targets are synchronized in explicit semantics can be helpful.

The issue of pastoral succession likewise surfaces in this matter. Yesterday when pastors changed, they moved their stuff and rearranged the rectory, period. Today new pastors most often enter an already numerous staff situation. Do they simply bless and continue what was? Do they change wholesale? I recall one situation in Ohio. The pastor was to be replaced. I met with three staff members. They told me they had built up a positive relationship with the present pastor. They were much concerned not only for the survival of their "jobs" but also for the complexities of developing a similar relationship with the new pastor. Succession, in short, has become a plural rather than a solo event. It is no longer merely a matter of two people shifting. Here too a good parish plan is helpful and a similar need for precise "skills and competences" is obvious.

Again, the pastor factor remains fundamental in parochial sharing and planning. But its application has much changed. Priests everywhere question how they may best accommodate these changes. Perhaps the advice given to another group of professionals is relevant:

> How do you stay professional? How do you stay vigilant? How do you maintain that razor's edge (and) meet the challenge of routine after years and years? . . . The routine is the enemy.[21]

If the priesthood is now "a specialized ministry," much prayer, training, patience, and continual readjustment is necessary. This entire text, again, provides the context in the sharing and planning dimension. Inertia, apathy, and pious platitudes cannot suffice. What is needed to reinvigorate and adapt the pastor factor in the contemporary parish is *a good comprehensive parish planning process beginning with an idealized design (dream) then surfacing an effective plan (and planlets) in which targets are collegially set and enthusiastically endorsed by the pastor, fleshed out with action detail and tactics by staff and appropriate advisory groups, then implemented in a carefully defined and*

designed system of strategies, roles, relationships, respon-
sibilities, and resource allocation—and periodically evalu-
ated and updated. If this is the corporate remedy, from a
personal point of view a pastor today requires a renewed
self-esteem and self-confidence. He needs also skills as an
interventionist. Consider:

A decade ago, a doctor expressed much self-confidence.
He noted:

> the absolute confidence I felt in the skill and intelligence of
> the people who had hold of me. In part this came from my
> own knowledge beforehand of their skill but in large part
> my confidence resulted from observing their own total con-
> fidence in themselves.[22]

Priests too, I suspect, once felt a similar confidence in
themselves, in those "who had hold" of them and in the
people they served. Today, on all counts, such confidences
have lessened. As he ages, the priest often experiences self-
doubts. Was I rightly prepared for the kind of ministry now
expected of me? I pray, I celebrate, but I must increasingly
deal in partnerships. I seem to have lost control of my tomorrows. The identity of the calling to which I dedicated my
entire being is now moot. Seminarians are few; not many
people will buy what is perceived to be a kind of pig in a
poke. Meanwhile, I'm not sure the Church above, my bishop
and our chancery, really care what I do. There is little evidence. And in the Church below, my congregation, there
is division and dissent. One principal objective in the proposed treatment of priesthood as a "specialized ministry"
must be to restore sacerdotal self-confidence in all dimensions.

Every pastor is an interventionist; in a divine sense, an
outrider from a kingdom not of this world; in a human sense,
a leadership person who proposes movement beyond inertia! Successful intervention requires a mix of "inspiration,
collaboration, sensitivity and organization."[23] More than

two decades ago, it was suggested that we knew little about how best to intervene:

> The role of the interventionist in our society is about where the role of the medical doctor was in the early 1700s.[24]

Even allowing for hyperbole then and much more sophistication now, intervention remains something which requires many "skills and competences." Here is one litany of its optimal ingredients:

> Leadership means vision, cheerleading, enthusiasm, love, trust, verve, passion, obsession, consistency, the use of symbols, paying attention . . . out and out drama, creating heroes at all levels, coaching, effectively wandering around and numerous other things.[25]

As he intervenes, the pastor like anyone else

> in the corporate world finds himself caught in a whirlwind of change, a world that focuses more on timely tasks than on timeless truths.[26]

Since his stock in trade is precisely such timeless truths, his situation is more difficult. We were told at the Massachusetts Institute of Technology that, as city planners, we would be required to reeducate ourselves several times from graduation to grave just to stay abreast of our profession. So too the intervening pastor must again and again rethink, relearn, and update his professional practices.

It is not the purpose of these pages to detail an andragogy for updating pastors. It is my purpose to suggest resources and to demonstrate that a good parish planning process can go far toward easing the task of parochial sharing and planning. For the rest, again, this entire text spotlights the "skills and competences" a good, lifelong learning pastor needs as he intervenes and enables his partner intervenors in a contemporary North American parish.

Finally, to reiterate the paramount urgency for on-site training and the willingness to be trained, the advice from business is clear:

Continuous improvement does not happen without continuous learning. . . . The key is action learning, working together in solving problems.[27]

The advice is just as loud and clear from under one of our busiest and apparently most effective steeples:

I believe we priests must continue our education just as physicians, attorneys, councillors, electricians, or anyone else must. If I needed surgery, would I approach a surgeon I know had not cracked a medical journal in ten years? No way. . . . Our competence does not come with our office or our ordination. We have to earn it as everyone else earns it.[28]

[1] Dr. Felix M. Lopez, consultant to many dioceses in the earliest days of American pastoral planning, to a convocation of Episcopalians, Florida, February 1973.

[2] Archbishop John May, St. Louis, April 11, 1989.

[3] Peter Black, *The Empowered Manager* (San Francisco: Jossey-Bass, 1987) 102.

[4] Shepherd's Care," National Conference of Catholic Bishops, 1987, 19, 29.

[5] David Peterson of Apple Computers, cited in James Kouzes and Barry Posner, *The Leadership Challenge* (San Francisco: Jossey-Bass, 1987) 21.

[6] Ibid., 71.

[7] "A Shepherd's Care," 9.

[8] Ibid., 19.

[9] Ibid., 43.

[10] Rev. Thomas F. Ventura, Chicago, in "The Parish in Transition," United States Catholic Conference, 1986, 50.

[11] Ibid., 52.

[12] Rev. Gerald F. Kicanis, CARA Seminary Forum, vol. 18 (spring 1990) 3.

[13] Rev. Leo B. Waynick, Jr., to convention of the National Pastoral Planning Conference, San Antonio, Texas, February 15, 1979.

[14] Rev. William J. Bausch, *Traditions, Tensions, Transitions in Ministry* (Mystic, Conn.: Twenty-Third Publications, 1982) 148.

[15] Ibid., 102.

[16] *Journal of the American Institute of Planners*, September 1967, Washington, D.C., 298.

[17] "A Shepherd's Care," 19.

[18] George M. Williams, *Improving Parish Management* (Mystic, Conn.: Twenty-Third Publications, 1983) 31.

[19] A top lay bank executive involved in his parish, cited in James H. Gollin, *Worldly Goods* (New York: Random House, 1971) 85.

[20] Amital Etzioni, *Modern Organizations* (Englewood, N.J.: Prentice-Hall, 1964) 79.

[21] T. Allan McArtor, then FAA chief, to two hundred pilots in Kansas City, *New York Times*, August 30, 1987, 6E.

[22] Lewis Thomas, *The Youngest Science: Notes of a Medicine Watcher* (New York: Viking, 1991) cited in "New York Times Review of Books," February 9, 1982, 25.

[23] "A Shepherd's Care," 18.

[24] Chris Argyris, *Management and Organization Development* (New York: McGraw Hill, 1971) 176.

[25] Tom Peters and Nancy Austin, *A Passion for Excellence* (New York: Random House, 1985) 6, 7.

[26] Garry Deweese, *Discipleship* 20 (1984) 1.

[27] C. Jackson Grayson and Carla O'Dell, *American Business: A Two Minute Warning* (New York: Free Press, 1988) 242.

[28] Robert D. Fuller, *Adventures of a Collegial Parish* (Mystic, Conn.: Twenty-Third Publications, 1981) 155.

CHAPTER FOURTEEN

COUNCIL CUES

> The parish pastoral council is the coordinating and unify-
> ing structure of the parish community. . . . The challenge
> of the Council is to integrate all the parishioners and group-
> ings into a body of people that functions as a commu-
> nity. . . . Every effort must be made to involve
> parishioners in the decisions that affect their own
> growth. . . . Clear, valuable and measurable goals are vi-
> tal for a parish. . . . To be successful, vision and goals must
> grow out of the needs of the entire parish and be claimed
> and worked on by all.[1]

As a parish shares and plans, its councillors are the point
people! They exemplify sharing at its local best. They cata-
lyze and sustain overall planning. True, pastoral councils
are now complemented by finance or administrative councils in most parishes. Suffice it on the next page to record
one good statement about the relationships which should
exist between them. Subsequently, here when I speak of
councils and councillors, I refer to parish pastoral councils.

Councils at all levels in diocesan polity are minimally
documented. There is little guidance from Vatican II, Canon
Law, etc. It would seem, however, that those words which
officially apply to diocesan pastoral councils can likewise
be invoked as one probes the polity of councils on the parochial level, e.g.:

(The Council is) to investigate all things pertaining to pastoral activity, to weigh them carefully and to set forth practical conclusions concerning them so as to promote conformity of the life and actions of the People of God with the Gospel ("Christus Dominus," Vatican II, sec. 27).

(It is the role of the Council) to offer its conclusions as to what is necessary for the diocesan community to organize the pastoral work and to efficiently execute it ("Directory on the Pastoral Ministry of Bishops," Sacred Congregation on the Clergy, 25 January 1973, sec. 4).

It also seems reasonable to apply on the parish council level what a recent national Church document said of the presbyteral council:

The council seeks information, evaluates that information, encourages those affected by the final decision to have a voice in the process, discusses the matter with the bishop and makes a recommendation to the bishop. The council, after studying the alternatives and the consequences of any proposed action, should make recommendations that are well thought out and feasible ("Presbyteral Councils," United States Catholic Conference/National Conference of Catholic Bishops, November 1991, pp. 436, 437).

There are local "guidelines." Most resonate the kind of thinking indicated above, for instance:

The parish council is the primary wisdom community of the parish, the place where the Gospel is clearly alive and well, the body which brings priests and lay leaders together in pastoral planning for the mission of the Church.[2]

Again and again the ideas and practices which I here recommend impact on and are impacted by parish councils. No need to repeat detail. Suffice it simpiy to highlight certain items of particular relevance to parish councillors as their parish proposes better ways to share and to plan:

1. SYNERGISTICS. This is the process through which parts are integrated in effective (performance + satisfaction)

Illustration 14.1

ANNUAL PARISH FINANCIAL PLANNING*

Person(s) Responsible	Task	Function
PASTORAL COUNCIL	Review MISSION of the church and Update NEEDS of the parish community	
	Establish GOALS and STRATEGIC PLAN	STRATEGIC PLANNING
	Establish PRIORITIES, PLANNING ASSUMPTIONS and GUIDELINES	
ADMINIS-TRATIVE COUNCIL	Establish OPERATIONAL PRIORITIES, Capital Projects, Space Needs, Personnel Positions, Equipment Needs	OPERATIONAL PLANNING
	REALLOCATE RESOURCES · in revising 3 YEAR PLAN	
	DEVELOP ANNUAL DETAILED BUDGET	RESOURCE ALLOCATION
PASTORAL COUNCIL	REVIEW annual budget and RECOMMEND APPROVAL to Pastor	
PASTOR	FINALIZE BUDGET	

*Excerpted from "Archdiocesan Administrative Manual," Archdiocese of Portland, Oregon, 1990, p. 30

wholes. *Synergistics* is the science of estimating, then interfacing multiple ingredients and factors in ongoing commonwealth. *I define planning as coherence plus energizing projection.* Synergy is another way of saying the same thing. A cohering council begins by canvassing current reality. Who now does what? What programs trend where? How best can these particular tentatives be melded into a coherent whole? A parallel between parochial and city councils suggests itself, though, obviously, the comparison limps. City councils hear recommendations from all city departments. Once a year they get agency budget requests. They then, to the best of their ability, adjudicate between persons and groups contending for limited city resources. Likewise, parochial councils are summoned to listen well, then measure each particular proposal in the light of planned priorities and limited resources. They are not city councils; they are not boards of directors. But in many ways their oversight function is similar. I admit that even the best council, at city hall or in the parish, often finds it difficult to tap in consistently to the feelings of its constituents. No other groups, however, are more qualified to attempt precisely this kind of overall representativity. Synergistics, to repeat, is commonwealth. Councillors are uniquely apt to accomplish this. But commonwealth will not and cannot happen until pastor and council converge to sustain it in the presence of often furious special interests, of insistent one note Joes and Janes!

2. PLAN. A good parish plan is synergistic. It records the best judgment of its pastor, staff, and people as to how this parish should best advance its several missions and ministries. A new sense of ownership and much enthusiasm have invigorated everyone. Relationships, once perhaps sporadic and difficult, have been explicitly regularized. Council agendas are projected ahead. Without a good plan, on the other hand, councils tend to drift.

Interest in them lags. There is no way to measure progress.

3. ASSEMBLY. This is an annual gathering of the parish to reflect on its planned mission and pastoral management and to suggest its future. Experience demonstrates that the continuous linkage of councils and pews is often otherwise ineffectual. "Open meetings" are sparsely attended. Councils may "report" once a year in the bulletin, but here too response is usually minimal. In the chapter "The Quantity Imperative," I recommend two procedural remedies. One is the frequent use of task forces. Suffice it here to explore the second remedy in greater detail—the annual parish assembly. Here are some of its benefits:

3.1 It provides a chance and a challenge to participate for parishioners who are unable or unwilling to share on a more frequent basis, e.g., as members of some eternal committee.

3.2 It provides a chance and a challenge for a council to inform and to be informed by its constituency face to face. A mere written "report" does not do this.

3.3 It provides a chance and a challenge for a council in a much larger forum to look at the parish not only in terms of specialist programs and particular needs but also in an overall dimension—and to do this both retrospectively and prospectively.

3.4 It provides a chance and a challenge in a parish with a pastoral plan to evaluate progress under this plan and to propose and detail future action.

3.5 It provides a unique opportunity for communal prayer, spiritual discernment, and recommitment. It is a visible sign of the unity of parishioners with their pastor, staff, and councillors,—and vice versa. (See also pages 32, 33.)

Thus, an assembly widens the sense of ownership on the part of a far larger constituency than can be engaged if the parish seems to be owned only by its pastor, staff, and a few local Medici!

SCYLLA/CHARYBDIS
In the middle stands virtue.

4. SAFE STEERING. An analogy from historic legendry! The ancients spoke of Scylla and Charybdis. On both sides of the narrow Straits of Messina between Italy and Sicily they saw immense danger for mariners. On one side, a siren, Scylla, lured sailors to their death. On the other side, a whirlpool, Charybdis, sank boats. The task was to safe-steer between them. The analogy is immensely apt in conciliar polity. There are advisors and doers in every parish. Councillors propose, pastors and staffs dispose. Inevitably, tensions arise. Some argue that such tensions can be defused if advisors confine themselves to "policy" while doers confine themselves to "program." Such a dictum reads well in books and at workshops. In practice it seldom happens as neatly! Take, for instance, an actual case in a large American diocese. Its DPC* had been conceived and practiced powerfully. It was suggested that this change. Henceforth, the DPC would deal only with policy and "long-range planning." Department heads would determine "programs." Proponents of change argued that the DPC had gotten mired down in actualities. It had not dreamed forward enough. Department heads complained of micro-management. Opponents contended that this change was a Trojan horse. It would push the DPC into platitudes. It could orate and project, but it would have little real impact on daily doings in the diocese. This case study indicates one of the problems which not infrequently surface in the relationship of advisors and doers. The subject is complex;

---

*Diocesan Pastoral Council.

there is much literature. I cannot begin to exhaust it here. From the advisory point of view, however, council status must repeatedly be questioned: Does this body really make a difference? Or, in this parish, do we experience two separate worlds? Councillors meet now and then on evenings and weekends, pastor and staff function with little interaction from nine to five on weekdays! Again, the Scylla/Charybdis analogy is apt.

4.1 For pastoral councils, *Scylla is the peril of platitude.* I call this sort of peril fluff stuff—or the "we-will-love-each-other-better-in-ten-years" syndrome! The council relaxes by choice, though often because it is forced to do so, in pious generalities. Nothing is ever specified. Nothing workable is enunciated. There are no evaluations because nothing the council suggests is measurable. Councils may occupy a bully pulpit but they make no matter! Often they just throw holy water on everything the parish now does. They rubber stamp staff. They may be guided by some kind of amorphous overall standards, but they fail to apply even these to ongoing parish persons and programs. They're irrelevant, marginal. They're nice people but they cut no ice. Fewer and fewer movers and shakers are attracted to them. As a result, they play trivial pursuits under their steeple. And, because they play trivial pursuits, fewer and fewer movers and shakers are attracted to them. A vicious circle indeed!

4.2 For pastoral councils, *Charybdis is the myopia of micro-management.* If the other extreme suggests a paper tiger council, at this extreme we speak of councils which are octopi. They meddle in everything. They are totally immersed in the here and now, in immediate detail. If they have an operating vision, this is a well-kept secret. Everything must be reported to such councils. They ride herd on every parish program, at least implying to the pastor that they could do it better.

Safe-steering between this Scylla and that Charybdis begins with the activation of two companion principles. The first, *subsidiarity*, suggests that so long as they act responsibly those who start particular programs should be given maximum autonomy by those in overall authority in the organizaion. But there is an equally if not even more urgent principle. I call it the principle of *pastoral wholeness.* Vatican II says it so—"a common effort to attain fullness in unity" ("Dogmatic Constitution of the Church," 13). Phrased otherwise:

> The central question in every pluralism has always been who takes care of the common good. . . . The flute part is an essential part of a Beethoven symphony but, by itself, it is not music.[3]

Thus, there is a difficult and delicate balance between the totality of mission and ministry and each expression of it. I submit from long experience that far too often in North American dioceses and parishes, subsidiarity is extensively practiced while wholeness repeatedly is aborted by rampant advocates on the one hand and authority unwilling to interfere with centrifugal inertia on the other hand. In parishes, far too often, particular groups are allowed to run with no overall guidance, while councils flounder unable judiciously to exercise their oversight function. Be all that as it may, a good parish plan provides a good council with a workable middle way between the Scylla of platitude and the Charybdis of micromanagement. Without it, not infrequently, councils tend to drift too close to one or another of these fatal extremes.

5. INTERNAL STRUCTURE. What kind of working committees and committees that work should a parish council have? Again, I recommend the frequent use of task forces to supplement eternal committees. Still, some such com-

mittees are appropriate. A parish like any other institution benefits from the continuity and group memory of this kind of group. There are various ways to proceed. I recommend to diocesan pastoral council start-up groups that they provide for only three DPC standing committees; I recommend likewise on the parish level. The first committee is, of course, *executive*. The second is *pastoral planning*; the third is *shared responsibility* or participation. I describe these as horizontal rather than the usual vertical committees. They spread in their special accountability over all programs and groups in the parish. Vertical committees, on the other hand, deal with particular items in mission and ministry, e.g,, school, liturgy. It may be necessary in some parishes to raise up a vertical committee where none now exists. By and large, I propose that the horizontal approach makes more practical sense. One advantage, to be brief, is that such an approach lessens the chance for friction, e.g., if there is a school board and the parish council likewise has an education committee.

6. PROCEDURE. There are several aspects to this, two rather obvious items to begin. First, to assure continuity and visible progress, all council recommendations should be numbered annually and their state, in terms of activation, modification, or rejection, should be reported back to the full council at the end of each work year. Second, council time is too precious, too brief, to be consumed with voluminous "reports"; and yet this often happens. My recommendation is that everyone who proposes to speak to the council be required to submit his/her report in writing to the council executive committee not less than a week prior to the meeting. This gives time to digest the report, perhaps even to mail it ahead to councillors. At the meeting, only critical items need to be vocally surfaced. In the place of a long-winded and self-righteous monologue, councillors are enabled to di-

alogue report content with the speaker. This is an important step forward from what now occurs in too many councils! The third procedural matter is more substantial and far more moot:

6.1 No one will dispute one thing: every advisory group should seek as much consensus as possible among its members and both with the authority and the constituency it serves. There is much disagreement as to how this can best be accomplished in a parish council. Some propose *Robert's Rules of Order;* and certainly one of the objectives of this orderly set of procedures is to foster workable consensus. Others propose what they call the *Consensus* method. They have developed a whole routine and rhythm. They suggest it is the best way to arrive at a pious consensus. Again, let it be clear; both approaches try to enable consensus. The idea itself cannot be claimed only by one of the contending methodologies. There are advantages and disadvantages either way. Suffice it to record my recommendations. If they lean more toward *Robert's Rules of Order*, this simply reflects the fact that proponents of *Consensus* have built up a greater head of steam for their approach. Thus, the possible defects in this approach need more insistently to be noted.

6.1.1 Church documents, while always promoting consensus, never in any way require that councils use either *Consensus* or *Robert's Rules of Order*. In fact, many ecclesial groups, including the American hierarchy when they meet, proceed with *Robert's Rules of Order*. In any case, *neither method should be or can be rightfully canonized.*

6.1.2 The theory behind both approaches is sound. But theory is often blighted in practice. For instance, when the Church promoted

Gregorian Chant! This was well done in workshops, by cathedral choirs, etc. When it hit the fan in most parishes, however, it was often far less expert. So too both *Robert's Rules of Order* and *Consensus* are brilliantly preached and nobly advocated. Their use in parishes is very often far less expert. Merely to invoke the ideal in either instance is not enough. One must canvass practice and then judge accordingly. It was thus, no doubt, that examining early experiences with MBO (management by objectives), revealed to its practical proponents that it often got lost in Papers and Process. So they changed it to MBO/R (management by objectives/results). Likewise, one valid and important test for *Robert's Rules of Order* and *Consensus* is which method better surfaces doable recommendations and precise conclusions from this council? Another test question: which method better enables this council to experience itself and be perceived as substantial and consequential, not just as a pious bull session?

6.1.3 It is often contended that there are "winners" and "losers" using *Robert's Rules of Order* but none in *Consensus*. This is simply not so. True, an improper use of *Robert's Rules of Order* can leave out-voted participants disgruntled; still these rules provide ample opportunity for input. And they assure that participants can, as appropriate, vote their consciences rather than run the guantlet of peer pressure by raising their hands. Besides, in an improper use of *Consensus*, peer pressure can be severe. And there can be losers in the sense that the ultimate recommendation is so watered down, so amorphous that it becomes in fact undoable. Thus participants see little evidence of consequences from their dialogue.

6.1.4 We went to the vernacular so people could understand what we did at our weekend altars. Americans are long since accustomed to *Robert's Rules of Order* when they convene. Far from being in any way unseemly, a good argument can be made that familiarity with these rules makes them even more appropriate when a council convenes.

6.1.5 A council should send clear and workable signals. Its role as a primary planning body in the parish requires that it do much more than speculate on generalities. Some argue that *Robert's Rules of Order* are much more amenable to a closed-ended result from council dialogue than is *Consensus*. Again, they base this view on practice in local parishes rather than on either approach as it is expertly preached and nobly advanced in academic places.

From all of the above, again, I recommend that neither *Robert's Rules of Order* nor *Consensus* be canonized. Perhaps, indeed, a judicious admixture of both is best!

As has been earlier noted, councillors propose, pastors and staffs dispose. There is much debate on how we have in fact practiced this critical but often difficult relationship. On the one hand:

> The wise chief executive knows that the greatest asset he has, over and above having a good strong management team, is a capable, interested, inquiring, and involved board of directors.[4]

On the other hand:

> There is no greater waste of human resources to be found in American corporations than the way boards of directors are typically used.[5]

Both views are probably correct. If executives in business and in civics have not figured out how best to set up and utilize their advisory groups, so too in the Church, there remains much uncertainty and imperfection. I know councils are not boards of directors, but the polity is in many ways similar. What should an advisory body be? A claque of official rubber stampers, pampered and anointed but inconsequential figureheads? Action intervenors? Somewhere in between? One thing, in my view, is sure: we have widely failed to give councils at all levels in the diocesan Church the attention and nurture they demand. If there is now a second spring for councils, in any case, I see few swallows. Diocesan council offices fall victim often to austerity or they are minimally staffed. There are few diocesan council newsletters; council leadership days are infrequent. The linkage in both directions between parochial, regional, and diocesan councils is too often ineffectual. And no one seems to care! Meanwhile, at least here and there, the ghost of "trusteeism" seems still to haunt conciliar polity.

Even, however, if its central and regional linkages and guidances are weak, each parish council is summoned to grow on local soil. There is much it can and should do. It is, for instance, charged to be realistic. It must be conversant in detail with parochial facts, feelings, and context. It must be hopeful, but not utopian. It must recognize its operational and advisory partners, always concerned to bring them together in one synergistic focus. It "safe steers" carefully between the Scylla of platitude and the Charybdis of micro-management. It is not merely babble and bravado. It is not just disembodied piety. Its fundamental task remains: (a) to canvass and assess all pastoral activities in the parish, (b) to discern spiritually and decide among alternative ways to make these activities more effective (performance + satisfaction), (c) to recommend its preferred alternatives in specific and systematic format to pastor and council, and then (d) to track and evaluate the course of its recommendations in the light of the parish plan. Let this suffice. For the rest, as with the pastor factor, everything in this text impacts on and is impacted by the parish council.

[1] "Parish Pastoral Council; Vision and Goals," Diocese of Joliet, Illinois, September 1990, 8, 9, 18, 19.

[2] Bishop Richard J, Sklba, "Living the Spirit," Archdiocese of Milwaukee, 1985, 1.

[3] Peter F. Drucker, *The New Realities* (New York: Harper and Row, 1989) 92, 96.

[4] J. Keith Louden, *The Effective Director in Action* (New York: American Management Association, 1975) 37.

[5] John O'Toole, *Vanguard Management* (New York: Berkley Publishing, 1987) 324, 325.

EPILOGUE

Everything has been said that I wanted and needed to say. Suffice it simply to append proof of my pudding!

Many parishes have in one way or another adopted my planning methodology. Two in particular have done what I consider to be effective plans. In each case, obviously, that methodology has been adjusted, for better or for worse, to local preferences. Still, by and large, the thrust is true.

One parish, St. Joseph, is located in Sykesville, Maryland. Its pastor is Rev. Thomas K. Cassidy, M.S. The other, St. Elizabeth Ann Seton, is located in Holmen, Wisconsin. Its pastor is Rev. Delbert Malin. I am grateful to these people and pastors for their permission to reproduce on the next pages portions of their respective plans. I look forward in the future to copies of other plans in which my RECKON ROAD has been followed.

Illustration E.1

St. Elizabeth Ann Seton, Holmen, Wisconsin (1991)

GOAL A: Develop and enhance the liturgical life of St.Elizabeth's Parish as celebrated in the Sacraments and other rites of the Church, with special attention to the devotional aspects of the Parish's prayer life and the liturgical ministries.

Priorities

MED   1. Increase the numbers of participants in each of the following liturgical ministries: Altar from 12 to 24; Eucharist from 114 to 128; Music from 56 to 62; Word from 50 to 55; and Hospitality from 105 to 120.
Responsibility: Sacred Worship Committee.
Target Date: Initiate actions to implement immediately; evaluate progress January 1992; accomplish November 1993.

HIGH   2. Establish a training program for Ministers of the Altar that includes at least four training sessions annually.
Responsibility: Sacred Worship Committee.
Target Date: November 1993.

H-M   3. Recruit and train three organists.
Responsibility: Sacred Worship Committee; Liturgical Ministers.
Target Date: November 1994.

MED   4. Increase Contemporary Choir by four members from 6 to 10.
Responsibility: Music Subcommittee; Liturgical Ministers
Target Date: November 1993.

MED   5. Form a liturgical drama group to be active at six children's liturgies and all major feast days.
Responsibility: Sacred Worship Committee; Education Committee
Target Date: Evaluate progress January 1992; accomplish by May 1993.

H-M   6. Offer one week-day evening Mass.
Responsibility: Pastor; Sacred Worship Committee.
Target Date: November 1992.

M-L   7. Establish a separate art and environment budget from the liturgical goods budget.
Responsibility: Sacred Worship Committee; Finance Council.
Target Date: July 1992.

St. Elizabeth Ann Seton, Holmen, Wisconsin (1991)

GOAL B: Foster Christian family life as central in all parish activities, including pastoral activities related to parish hospitality, social activities, vocations, marriage preparation and enrichment, and the pastoral care of single adult Catholics and the elderly.

Priorities

HIGH   1. Develop a newcomers' program consisting of a parish welcome, home visitation, information on the parish, and introduction to current members.
Responsibility: Family Life Committee; PCCW and KCs.
Target Date: June 1993.

a. Prepare an information flyer.
Responsibility: Family Life Committee; Parish Staff.
Target Date: September 1991.

b. Develop a group of 10 active members to do home visitations.
Responsibility: Family Life Committee; Parish Staff.
Target Date: November 1992.

c. Recognize newcomers at Mass by having them stand and be introduced.
Responsibility: Family Life Committee; Pastor.
Target Date: September 1991.

M-H   2. Conduct two marriage encounters in the Holmen-Onalaska parishes each year.
Responsibility: Family Life Committee; Parish Staff.
Target Date: June 1993.

M-H   3. Develop two marriage encounter teams, each consisting of three couples.
Responsibility: Family Life Committee; Parish Staff.
Target Date: June 1992.

HIGH   4. Develop a senior citizen program for the older members of our parish which includes at least two events in the first year.
Responsibility: Family Life Committee.
Target Date: September 1992.

HIGH   5. Conduct two family-centered social activities in the parish each year.
Responsibility: PCCW; KCs; Family Life Committee
Target Date: September 1992

Illustration E.2

St. Joseph, Sykesville, Maryland

CRITICAL PASTORAL CONCERN AREAS
October 21, 1987

The Administrative Staff of St. Joseph's proposes the following list of Critical Pastoral Concern Areas.

Ref. No.

1 SPIRITUAL LIFE
Liturgy, music, retreat-mission and renewal processes, evangelization, Christian initiation, spiritual direction, ecumenism, development of religious and lay vocation and ministry.

2 PARISH COMMUNITY
Social activities, sports, hospitality, small faith communities, all parochial organizations except Parish Council assemblies.

3 FAMILY LIFE
Sacramental preparation and enrichment, marriage encounter, pre-Cana, family life programs, youth ministry, pastoral counseling, ministry to young adults, ministry to the elderly.

4 FAITH EDUCATION
Christian formation at all age levels, participation in regional Catholic school endeavor, formation resources.

5 SOCIAL ACTION
Respect life, pro-life, prophecy, justice and peace, outreach to the poor, civic and inter-parochial social witness, advocacy, health ministry.

6 PLANNING
Discernment, planned continuity, parish council, relating with the archdiocese and regional council.

7 MANAGEMENT
Administration, finances, facilities.

Illustration E.3

St. Joseph, Sykesville, Maryland

1/14/88   **OBJECTIVE REPORT**

CRITICAL PASTORAL CONCERN AREA NO.: 2
         Objective Start Date: 2/01/88
PARISH COMMUNITY   Objective Completion Date: 2/28/89

GOAL NO.: 2001
     TO ESTABLISH AT LEAST HOST FAMILY IN 80% OF THE
     COMMUNITY DESIGNATED AREAS BY 2/28/91

OBJECTIVE NO.: 1
     DEFINE THE "HOST" PROGRAM FOR ST. JOSEPH'S AND
     IMPLEMENT SAME IN 10% OF DESIGNATED PARISH
     AREAS.

1. RESPONSIBILITY OF: P&CR, Host Committee

2. PARISH COUNCIL ROLE:

3. RESOURCES

Item Required in Program/Project	Person Hours	Facilities	Funds
3.1 Organizational meetings	50	Homes	0.00
3.2 Recruit & train Hosts	100	VCR	125.00
3.3 Publicize Host Program		Printer	700.00
3.4 Home visits & handout distribution	1500		1,200.00
		Objective Cost:	2,025.00

NOTES:

4. TASK SEQUENCE

Step	Completed by
4.1 Recruit core members	2/29/88
4.2 Recruit Hosts and train	5/31/88
4.3 Implement in 10% of parish areas	9/30/88
4.4 Evaluate and modify as necessary	12/31/88

5. COMMENTS
1st of 3 objectives to accomplish 80% participation of communities in the Host program.

St. Joseph, Sykesville, Maryland

2/13/88   **OBJECTIVE REPORT**

CRITICAL PASTORAL CONCERN AREA NO.: 4

Objective Start Date: 8/01/88
FAITH EDUCATION   Objective Completion Date: 5/31/89

GOAL NO.: 4201
TO IMPLEMENT A "TOTAL YOUTH MINISTRY" COMPOSED OF TEENS, YOUNG ADULTS, AND ADULTS ACTIVELY INVOLVED IN YOUTH MINISTRY

OBJECTIVE NO.: 9
TO COLLABORATE WITH THE FAMILY COMMITTEE IN ASSISTING THE YOUTH IN FULLY PLANNING AND EXECUTING FOUR LITURGY CELEBRATIONS.

1. RESPONSIBILITY OF: PALM & PAYM

2. PARISH COUNCIL ROLE:

3. RESOURCES

Item Required in Program/Project	Person Hours	Facilities	Funds
3.1 Schedule facilities	1	Church	0.00
3.2 VCR	2	Classroom	0.00
3.3 Musical instruments	2	Church	0.00
3.4 Planning	40		50.00
		Objective Cost:	50.00

NOTES:

4. TASK SEQUENCE

Step	Completed by
4.1 Recruit Youth	8/31/88
4.2 Plan liturgies	8/31/88
4.3 Lector training	11/30/88
4.4 Music practice	1 week prior to liturgy

5. COMMENTS
The intent here is to help youth participate more fully in the Sunday liturgy by: 1) executing various liturgical ministries available to them and 2) publically witnessing their liturgical skills to other youth in the parish.

Illustration E.4

St. Joseph, Sykesville, Maryland (1991)

July 1991–June 1992

PARISH WIDE GOALS AND OBJECTIVES

COLLABORATION: St. Joseph's has become a collaborative community which has functioning a networking of the various ministries so that there is a system for understanding, communicating and networking together.

OBJECTIVE 1:   Commission Chairpersons will review with their commissions the goals and objectives from the All-Day Parish Council Planning Meeting to look for places of collaboration with other commissions.

OBJECTIVE 2:   The Parish Council will make a commitment to include an opportunity for mutual sharing at each parish council gathering.

OBJECTIVE 3:   On June 8, 1991, the Parish Council Executive Board will sponsor a breakfast for all commission heads, committee chairmen, elected Parish Council members and staff to share enthusiasms and ideas.

OBJECTIVE 4:   Parish Leaders will more frequently use the pronouns "we," "us," and "our," rather than "they," "them," or "their" in discussing Parish activities and processes.

In describing parishioners' participation, the use of the term "volunteer" will discontinue in favor of naming the service provided or the ministerial role.

OBJECTIVE 5:   The Spiritual Journey Committee will sponsor a yearly retreat for Parish Leaders centered on the Mission Statement.

OBJECTIVE 6:   The Parish Mission Statement will be the focus of a day of retreat at our parish facilities for parish council members and other parish leadership, planned by the Spiritual Journey Committee for late Lent, 1992.

OBJECTIVE 7:   Delegates of Parish Council will be willing to meet with any individual or group when invited.

Illustration E.5

St. Joseph, Sykesville, Maryland (1991)

Pastoral Plan

COMMISSION GOALS AND OBJECTIVES

CHRISTIAN SERVICE

Goal 1: Increase parish awareness and involvement in Christian Service Ministries

- Education programs by CS Commission on Church and Social Issues; specifically, Third World, Respect Life, Health ministry, and Catholic Social Teaching.
- Each CS committee to address the RCIA to educate and to invite candidates' participation.
- The Parish is invited to two educational meetings on Respect Life issues each year.
- Hold at least 4 Parish Prayer Vigils for Life per year.
- Promote a letter writing campaign for Respect Life Issues which will involve the entire parish.
- Sponsor teachers to educate CYO, 7th, and 8th graders on life, crisis pregnancy, abortion issues.
- Arrange for and support parish members to visit Latin American Partner Parishes and report back to the parish and other groups on their experience.
- Prepare brochure for handouts, inserts, and Welcome Table.
- Prepare series of petitions for use in Prayer of Faithful.
- Expand use of term, "Partners in Faith" instead of common use of "Sister Parish" when referring to Third Worlds Concerns Committee (TWCC) parish relationships.
- Parish Council Members and Commission Members are encouraged to make more referrals to Stephen Peer Ministry.

Goal 2: Expand existing Christian Service Ministries to include the wider community and other parishes.

- Each Committee will have made contact with a related group in the local or regional area to collaborate efforts by June 1992.
- Establish a liaison between our parish and the Maryland Legislature to keep abreast of particular social issues.

- Prison Ministry Team will establish an ongoing relationship between itself and the Unity Methodist Church in Baltimore City so that Central Laundry prisoners may be supported through outreach ministries.
- Prison Ministry team will recruit at least 2 members in calendar year 1991 to support and administer, as required, in its relationship among the Unity Methodist Church, Central Laundry prisoners (and ex-prisoners) and the Prison Ministry Team.

St. Joseph Catholic Community